History

FOR THE IB DIPLOMA

Keely Rogers
Jo Thomas

OXFORD
UNIVERSITY PRESS

OXFORD
UNIVERSITY PRESS

Great Clarendon Street, Oxford OX2 6DP

Oxford University Press is a department of the University of Oxford.
It furthers the University's objective of excellence in research,
scholarship, and education by publishing worldwide in

Oxford   New York

Auckland Cape Town Dar es Salaam Hong Kong Karachi
Kuala Lumpur Madrid Melbourne Mexico City Nairobi
New Delhi Shanghai Taipei Toronto

With offices in

Argentina Austria Brazil Chile Czech Republic France Greece
Guatemala Hungary Italy Japan Poland Portugal Singapore
South Korea Switzerland Thailand Turkey Ukraine Vietnam

Oxford is a registered trade mark of Oxford University Press
in the UK and in certain other countries

British Library Cataloguing in Publication Data

Data available

ISBN: 978-0-19-839014-5
10 9 8 7 6 5 4 3 2 1

Printed in Malaysia by Vivar Printing Sdn. Bhd.

Paper used in the production of this book is a natural, recyclable product made
from wood grown in sustainable forests. The manufacturing process conforms
to the environmental regulations of the country of origin

Acknowledgments

This material has been developed independently by the publisher and the content
is in no way connected with nor endorsed by the International Baccalaureate
Organization.

Cover image by David Lawrence; **p11:** Kateryna Upit/Shutterstock; **p12t:** Diego
Cervo/Shutterstock; **p12b:** Monkey Business Images/Shutterstock; **p18tr:** Michael
Marsland/Yale University office of Public Affairs & Communications; **p18b:** published
by Jonathan Cape/Reprinted by permission of The Random House Group Ltd; **p19:**
Woodrow Wilson International Center for Scholars; **p20:** Associated Press/Press
Association Images; **p26:** www.cartoons.ac.uk/Associated Newspapers Ltd/Solo
Syndication; **p27:** Associated Newspapers Ltd/Solo Syndication; **p28:** www.cartoons.
ac.uk/© Guardian News & Media Ltd 1967; **p29:** www.cartoons.ac.uk/Nicholas
Garland; **p36:** www.cartoons.ac.uk/© Telegraph Media Group Limited 1967; **p37:**
Topical Press Agency/Getty Images; **p53:** Punch Limited/TopFoto; **p54:** www.cartoons.
ac.uk/Associated Newspapers Ltd/Solo Syndication; **p56:** www.cartoons.ac.uk/
Nicholas Garland; **p58:** Lisa F. Young/Shutterstock; **p77:** Stan Eales/www.CartoonStock.
com; **p79:** Frank and Helena/Alamy; **p101:** David H. Lewis/iStockphoto; **p103:**
Superstudio/Getty Images; **p121:** Frihedsmuseet (Museum of Danish Resistance
1940 -1945); **p124:** iStockphoto/Thinkstock; **p130:** Wavebreak Media Ltd/Alamy;
p131: aldegonde le compte/Alamy; **p132:** Anton Prado/Shutterstock; **p133:** Jon
Kudelka/Kudelka Cartoons; **p137:** imagebroker/Alamy; **p138:** Topham Picturepoint/
Press Association Images; **p140:** The National Women's History Project; **p142:**
published by Pimlico/Reprinted by permission of The Random House Group Ltd;
p144tr: Niday Picture Library/Alamy; **p144l:** Robin Weaver/Alamy; **p144m:** Colouria
Media/Alamy; **p144b:** Archivesdu7eArt/DR/Photo12.com; **p145:** TOLES © 2010 The
Washington Post/Reprinted with permission of UNIVERSAL UCLICK. All rights
reserved; **p149:** Dan Piraro/Bizarro.

Illustrations by Adam Nickel

The authors and publisher are grateful for permission to reprint extracts from the
following copyright material:

To the International Baccalaureate Organization for permission to reproduce its
intellectual property.

J Black & D Macraild: from *Studying History* (Palgrave Study Skills, 3e, 2007),
reprinted by permission of Palgrave Macmillan.

Louise Doder: 'A Bloodbath in Beijing', *Maclean's*, 12 June 1989, copyright © 1989
by Maclean Hunter Ltd, reprinted by permission of Maclean's Magazine.

Sir Antony Eden: from *Full Circle (Memoirs)* (Cassell, 1960), reprinted by permission
of the Estate.

R J Evans: from *In Defence of History* (Granta, 1997), reprinted by permission of
Granta Books and The Wylie Agency for the author.

Orlando Figes: from *A People's Tragedy: The Russian Revolution 1891- 1924* (Jonathan
Cape, 1996), copyright © Orlando Figes 1996, reprinted by permission of The
Random House Group Ltd and Viking Penguin, a division of Penguin Group (USA) inc.

Jack Gray: from *Rebellions and Revolutions: China from the 1800s to the 1980s* (OUP, 1990),
reprinted by permission of Oxford University Press.

Immanuel C Y Hsu: from *The Rise of Modern China* (6e, OUP, 2000), reprinted by
permission of Oxford University Press.

K Jenkins: from *Rethinking History* (Routledge, 1991, n/e 2003) , reprinted by

permission of Taylor & Francis Books/Cengage Learning (EMEA) Ltd.

Donald Justice: lines from 'Pantoum of the Great Depression', from *Collected Poems*
(Alfred Knopf, 2004/ Anvil, 2006), copyright © 2004 Donald Justice, reprinted by
permission of Anvil Press Poetry and Alfred A Knopf, a division of Random House,
Inc.

John Maynard Keynes: from *The Collected Writings of John Maynard Keynes, Vol. 2: The
Economic Consequences of the Peace* (Macmillan, London for the Royal Economic Society,
1971), reprinted by permission of Palgrave Macmillan.

W Lefeber, R Polenberg and N Woloch: *The American Century: A History of the
United States Since 1941* (4th Edition, McGraw Hill, 1992), reprinted by permission of
The McGraw-Hill Companies.

Michael Lynch: from *The People's Republic of China 1949-1976* (Hodder, 2008), reprinted
by permission of the publishers.

Frank McDonough: from *Hitler, Chamberlain and Appeasement* (Cambridge University
Press 2002), reprinted by permission of the publisher.

Harold Nicolson: from *Peacemaking 1919* (Constable & Co, 1933), copyright ©
Harold Nicolson, 1933, reprinted by permission of Curtis Brown Group Ltd, London
on behalf of the Estate of Harold Nicolson.

R Overy: from *Why the Allies Won* (Pimlico, 2006), reprinted by permission of The
Random House Group Ltd and Rogers, Coleridge & White Ltd, 20 Powis Mews,
London W11 1JN,

Kirsten E Schulze: from *Arab-Israeli Conflict* (2e, Pearson Longman, 2008), reprinted
by permission of Pearson Education.

Charles D Smith: from *Palestine and the Arab-Israeli Conflict* (St Martin's Press, 1988/
Palgrave Macmillan, 2004), reprinted by permission of Palgrave Macmillan.

Barry Turner: from *Suez, the Inside Story of the First Oil War* (Hodder & Stoughton,
2006), reprinted by permission of the publishers

Zhang Gong: statement from 'State Council Spokesman Yuan Mu Holds News
Conference', originally from Foreign Broadcast Information Service (FBIS), 7.6.1989,
published in M Oksenberg, L R Sullivan and Marc Lambert (eds.): *Beijing, Spring 1989:
Confrontation and Conflict - The Basic Documents* (ME Sharpe, 1990), translation copyright
© 1990 by M E Sharpe Inc, reprinted by permission of the publishers.

We have tried to trace and contact all copyright holders before publication. If
notified, the publishers will be pleased to rectify any errors or omissions at the
earliest opportunity.

Contents

Introduction

History and the IB learner profile

As an IB history student, you will have the opportunity to develop an indepth knowledge of different aspects of 20th-century history from different regions of the world. If you are doing higher level (HL) history, then you may be studying 19th-century topics as well.

This is an exciting prospect; it will mean that by the time you have completed your diploma you will have a greater understanding of the world in which you live. Indeed, one of the aims of the IB Diploma Programme history course is to encourage you to develop the characteristics of IB learners; that is, 'internationally minded people who, recognizing their common humanity and shared guardianship of the planet, help to create a better and more peaceful world' (*IB Diploma Programme History guide*, March 2008). Your development as an IB learner will be helped and encouraged through the study of history.

What skills do you need as an IB history student?

In order to get the most from your history studies and to ensure that you also receive the best grades possible, you will have to work hard to develop certain skills. Indeed, as a history student you face a demanding task. Not only do you have to read and learn the factual information for your topics, you then have to make sure you understand this information so that you can analyse and evaluate it.

The kind of skills you need to develop can be linked to Bloom's taxonomy of different kinds of learning. Bloom saw the top of the pyramid as representing the highest level - and this is ultimately what you will need to do in your essay writing and source work. However, the bottom of the pyramid – knowledge and comprehension – provides the basis for all of the higher levels. You cannot demonstrate one with out the other!

If you refer to the *IB Diploma Programme History guide*, March 2008, pg. 8, you will see that these skills are the basis for your assessment objectives. Knowledge and understanding are assessment objective 1, application and interpretation are assessment objective 2 and synthesis and evaluation are assessment objective 3. Assessment objective 4, use of historical skills, encompasses all areas in the pyramid on the next page.

In addition to working on your ability to analyse and evaluate, you also need to be able to present your conclusions in a structured way that clearly answers any question that the examiners may set you. All of this will require not just a love of history and a desire to find out about the past, but also good study skills, an ability to think things through, and the skill of communicating effectively.

These skills will help you in a broad range of other IB subjects and will be applicable to any higher education courses that you take. They will also prepare you for a range of careers that need these skills. Your ability to extract relevant information from a wide range of sources, to analyse that information, to present different arguments, to reach conclusions and to communicate all of this effectively will give you a skill set that employers value highly. For example, history students go on to careers in journalism, law, marketing, sales, banking, management, teaching, computing and politics.

Bloom's taxonomy

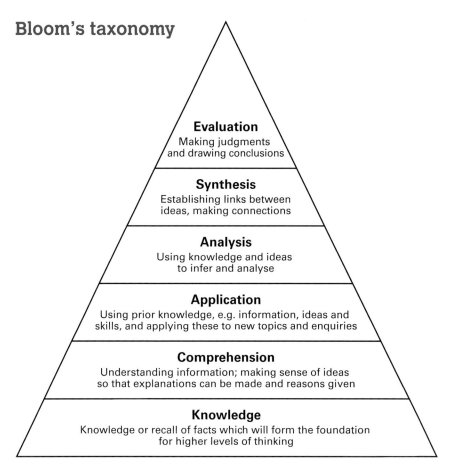

Evaluation
Making judgments and drawing conclusions

Synthesis
Establishing links between ideas, making connections

Analysis
Using knowledge and ideas to infer and analyse

Application
Using prior knowledge, e.g. information, ideas and skills, and applying these to new topics and enquiries

Comprehension
Understanding information; making sense of ideas so that explanations can be made and reasons given

Knowledge
Knowledge or recall of facts which will form the foundation for higher levels of thinking

Evaluation, synthesis and analysis are the skills that you need to get the top levels in essay writing

Although it is the 'lowest' level on Bloom's Taxonomy, knowledge is key for all historians - you will not be able to write good essays without having a strong knowledge base!

The structure of this book

The aim of this book is to help you achieve the skills discussed above and to help you to become a successful IB history student. It is divided into the following sections.

Key skills

This section of the book looks at the basic skills that you need as a starting point for any historical investigation. This includes finding relevant information and how to read effectively and take notes. It will also look at the range of historical sources that you will come across in your studies and the value and limitations of using these different sources.

Document analysis and essay writing

Key to your success in the IB examination is an understanding of what is required in each of the different parts of the examination. For this reason, the second section of this book looks at how you apply your history skills to the IB history examination in Papers 1, 2 and 3 and what exactly is required for each section of the examination. We will give help on how to answer questions for Paper 1 and to how to write essays for Papers 2 and 3.

Individual assignment (IA) and extended essay

The third and fourth sections explore in more detail the skills and process of writing the IA and the extended essay in history.

Revision skills

The fifth section of the book outlines the skills you will need to revise for the examination and suggests strategies to help you with revision.

Activity

The aims of the history course at standard level and higher level (SL and HL) are to:

- promote an understanding of history as a discipline, including the nature and diversity of its sources, methods and interpretations
- encourage an understanding of the present through critical reflection on the past
- encourage an understanding of the impact of historical developments at national, regional and international levels
- develop an awareness of one's own historical identity through the study of the historical experiences of different cultures (*IB Diploma Programme history guide*, March 2008, pg. 7).

Look at the characteristics of an IB learner. How might the study of history help in your quest to become an IB learner?

The IB Learner Profile

It is the goal of all IB programmes to develop internationally minded people who work to create a better and more peaceful world. The aim of the programme is to develop this person through ten learner attributes, as described below.

Inquirers: They develop their natural curiosity. They acquire the skills necessary to conduct inquiry and research and snow independence in learning. They actively enjoy learning and this love of learning will be sustained throughout their lives.

Knowledgeable: They explore concepts, ideas, and issues that have local and global significance. In so doing, they acquire in-depth knowledge and develop understanding across a broad and balanced range of disciplines.

Thinkers: They exercise initiative in applying thinking skills critically and creatively to recognize and approach complex problems, and make reasoned, ethical decisions.

Communicators: They understand and express ideas and information confidently and creatively in more than one language and in a variety of modes of communication. They work effectively and willingly in collaboration with others.

Principled: They act with integrity and honesty, with a strong sense of fairness, justice and respect for the dignity of the individual, groups and communities. They take responsibility for their own action and the consequences that accompany them.

Open-minded: They understand and appreciate their own cultures and personal histories, and are open to the perspectives, values and traditions of other individuals and communities. They are accustomed to seeking and evaluating a range of points of view, and are willing to grow from the experience.

Caring: They show empathy, compassion and respect towards the needs and feelings of others. They have a personal commitment to service, and to act to make a positive difference to the lives of others and to the environment.

Risk-takers: They approach unfamiliar situations and uncertainty with courage and forethought, and have the independence of spirit to explore new roles, ideas, and strategies. They are brave and articulate in defending their beliefs.

Balanced: They understand the importance of intellectual, physical and emotional balance to achieve personal well-being for themselves and others.

Reflective: They give thoughtful consideration to their own learning and experience. They are able to assess and understand their strengths and limitations in order to support their learning and personal development.

from *IB learner profile booklet* © International Baccalaureate Organization 2006

Key skills for the study of history at IB

In this section we look at the core skills you will need for all parts of the examination.

Finding information

Your starting point in learning about a new topic, whether for an essay, your IA or extended essay, is usually through reading and, as an IB history student, you will have to read a wide range of texts and sources.

Before you start reading, you must be clear in your mind what information you are looking for. This will determine your choice of books and also keep you focused when reading.

In your IB history class you will be expected to read and make notes from textbooks. Your teacher may supplement this with extra handouts such as articles or extracts from historians, and will probably give you guidelines on what to look for. As such, you will have a clear idea on what to read and on what you looking for in your reading.

The task of reading becomes more challenging when preparing to write your IA or extended essay for IB history. Here you will have to be more independent in your choice of texts.

So where do you start?

The key rule is always to move from the general to the particular and from the simple to the complex.

If you are investigating the causes of the terror under Stalin, for example, you could follow the following structure.

Type of reading	Purpose	Example
1 General text	A straightforward overview text will give you an introduction to the topic and allow you to put it into historical context.	Evans, D. and Jenkins, J., 2001, *Years of Russia, the USSR and the Collapse of Soviet Communism*, London: Hodder and Stoughton.
2 Specialized text	This will be detailed with weightier analysis and will help you identify key issues on your topic. The bibliography may also lead you to other useful sources.	Montefiore, S., 2004, *Stalin: The court of the Red Tsar*, New York: Knopf.
3 Articles	An article will be a succinct summary of one particular issue, written by a historian to provide an update on his or her research or as a contribution to a journal, book or website. An article is very useful for giving you a concise, up-to-date viewpoint of a key point or argument.	Ilic, M., 'The Great Terror reassessed', *20th Century History Review*, April 2006.
4 Primary documents	These include contemporary sources such as speeches, diaries and memoirs. You will find it interesting and useful to read some of these for your IA or extended essay to give you a more in-depth understanding of your topic.	Various, for example from www.hoover.org/publications/hoover-digest/article/6897

Techniques for reading

Do not start by trying to read in detail every source from the first page – you need to develop a range of reading techniques to suit your different purposes. You may begin by scanning, for example, and then move on to detailed reading.

Scanning

This is useful technique to get an overall perspective of a book or article and to find if it is relevant to your needs. It involves moving your eyes quickly over the page to indentify relevant words or topics.

Particularly important are the introduction of the book, the first and last paragraphs of chapters and the concluding chapter, as these should summarize the key ideas. With shorter texts, such as articles, scan over the first sentences of paragraphs to establish the key points.

Skimming

This is to get the gist of the main points of the book or article and involves focusing on the main points only while 'skimming over' the detail. This is useful to get the main ideas before you read for detail.

Detailed reading

This is when you read every word of the text. This will be necessary to get the detail that you need to support your arguments. Sometimes you will need to read key sections more than once.

By 1960... the Chinese had begun to believe that too great a dependence on Russia would simply inhibit China's own attempts to improve her position.

Two further events confirmed China's worst fears. The first was the Cuban crisis in 1962 when Khrushchev, after attempting to install rocket bases in Cuba, backed down in the face of American threats, saving his face by procuring from Washington a promise that America would not invade Cuba, an action which, in view of the farcical failure of the recent Bay of Pigs venture, the United States was very unlikely to attempt again. The Chinese took much the same view of the Cuban crisis as the rest of the world. They condemned Khrushchev for his dangerously provocative act, which could bring no advantage commensurate with its risks, and they held him in contempt for his subsequent pusillanimous withdrawal. Their conclusion was that the Soviet Union under Khrushchev could not even consistently pursue its own policy of co-existence.

The second was the Test Ban Treaty, concluded in 1963 by the Soviet Union and the United States. In effect it sought to bestow a monopoly of nuclear arms on those powers which already possessed them. The Chinese regarded the Treaty as aimed mainly at China. Further, they regarded it as decisive proof that the two superpowers were being drawn, however reluctantly, into the creation of a worldwide diarchy. It was at this point that the Chinese broke openly with the Soviet Union.

Grey, J., 1990, *Rebellions and Revolutions: China from the 1800s to the 1980s*, Oxford University Press, pg. 324.

What key points has the student identified concerning the reasons for the breakdown of Sino-Soviet relations?

Active reading

It is important to be an 'active' reader in order to maintain your concentration and to develop your understanding. Follow the points below to help achieve this.

Some practical points

Tip

These are a few key words and phrases used by historians to identify their main points.

Fundamental, key, crucial

Led to...

Was the result of...

A turning point was...

Moreover,...

The most important (cause or result...) was...

It is obvious that...

Furthermore,...

Make sure that you are clear on the questions that you want to answer from your reading

Highlight or underline key points

Also draw up timelines; this will help you not only get the chronology of events sorted out but will help you to identify the importance of certain years, and where there are turning points

Check any vocabulary that you are not sure about – check glossaries and keep a dictionary to hand

Notice headings, italics and bold face in the text which are there to emphasize points and may help you with structuring your own notes

Write notes after each section of the text (see next section)

Do you agree with everything? Does this account contradict any views you have already read? Be prepared to reflect on points made by historians and the evidence used to support their ideas

Note taking: the essentials

When studying IB history, you will be confronted with various sources of information: from textbooks, articles, historians, DVDs, internet resources or from your teacher talking.

Taking notes from these sources is essential for several reasons.

- Notes help you to get the most from your lessons; you have to concentrate, listen and organize the main points that are being made. This makes you an active participant in the learning process. By sorting out what is important and what is not important, you are also starting to comprehend and to analyse what is being said.
- Similarly, if you take notes when reading, you are more actively involved in the learning process, synthesizing the information and deciding on key points to record. Note taking will also help you to remember what you read; without it, there is a good chance that your reading will have been a waste of time.
- A good set of notes from a range of sources will form the basis for your essay writing, your IA and extended essay.
- Notes form the basis for your revision for tests and the IB examination.

The process of note taking

Taking notes is a very individual process and you need to work out the best way for you to take notes. You may also find that you use different types of notes for different learning purposes (for example when preparing for an essay and learning for an examination) and for different subject matter.

Note taking from a text

Be clear about your purpose before you start taking notes – what are you looking for? Is it a factual account of an event, a historian's view of an event or both?

Start by scanning the chapter or article to find out what it is about; decide, as you are scanning whether it is of any use to your purpose.

Assuming that the text is useful, skim read to get the gist of the key arguments or detail. Then reread for detail, taking notes as you do so. (You may want to highlight key points as a prelude to taking notes.)

Bear these points in mind as you take notes.

- Try to distinguish between straightforward facts and analysis of those facts. You need to know the basic facts or narrative but your essays will require **analysis**, that is a focus on **why** something happened or the **consequences** or **connections** between events or the **importance** of the actions of a person.
- Use your own words but make sure that you are accurate (take particular care with proper names and new vocabulary).
- Be concise; resist the temptation to include too much. Omit descriptions and full explanations.
- Include details of dates and statistics – these are key to providing clear evidence to any argument.
- Write out useful quotations – they should be short and punchy. Before doing so decide whether the quotation is saying something in a way that you would not be able to match for style and eloquence. If you **can** match its style and eloquence, then rewrite the quotation in your own words.

Activity

1 Read the text below, which is discussing the question: **How effective was the Allied bombing campaign against Germany and Japan in the Second World War?**

As you read,

- highlight the factual information in the text, for example what are the key dates? Are there any statistics that are useful as evidence on this issue?

- highlight in a different colour the parts of the text that go beyond factual information and provide analysis or opinion on the issue

- look out for any quotes that might be useful.
  (See the tip on using highlighters.)

2 Next make notes based on your highlighted areas of reading. You may want to use one of the styles of note taking suggested on pages 13–15.

3 Compare your notes with those of a partner. Find one point that your partner has included that you have not included (and vice versa). How were your styles of note taking similar or different?

Tip

Using highlighters

Many students like to highlight key points in a text while reading. This is important to help you develop 'saliency determination' – the ability to discriminate between important and unimportant information.

This is a good technique to use as a starting point to making notes.

Remember, though, that this is not the end of the process. Having highlighted key points, these then need to be written down into a coherent set of notes.

There has always seemed something fundamentally implausible about the contention of bombing's critics that dropping almost 2.5 million tons of bombs on tautly-stretched industrial systems and war-weary urban populations would not seriously weaken them. Germany and Japan had no special immunity. Japan's military economy was devoured in the flames; her population desperately longed for escape from bombing. German forces lost half of the weapons needed at the front, millions of workers absented themselves from work, and the economy gradually creaked almost to a halt. Bombing turned the whole of Germany, in Speer's words, into a 'gigantic front'. It was a front the Allies were determined to win; it absorbed resources on both sides. It was a battlefield in which only the infantry were missing. The final victory of the bombers in 1944 was, Speer concluded, 'the greatest lost battle on the German side…'. Though there should be necessary arguments over the morality or operational effectiveness of the bombing campaigns, the air offensive appears in fact as one of the decisive elements in explaining Allied victory.'

Overy, R., 2006, *Why the Allies Won,* London: Pimlico (Random House), pg. 163.

Note taking from a teacher or lecturer

This is definitely trickier – you cannot go at your own pace. We would hope that there is a clear theme to the lesson and notes on a whiteboard or PowerPoint that will help you to identify the key points and give you a structure. However, there are also ways in which you can help yourself.

- Make sure that you are prepared for class and that you have reviewed the previous lesson or read anything set by the teacher to prepare you for the session – the more you know what is going on, the more you will be able to identify the key points and understand the key issues involved.
- Be attentive! Getting used to the voice and gestures of the lecturer should help you identify when that person is stressing a key point. There should also be 'signal statements' to alert you to a key point, for example 'The most important point is…' or 'Don't forget that…'.
- You will need to write quickly and so developing abbreviations for key words will help you (see page 16).
- After the lesson read your textbook to consolidate what you have covered in class – this will also help you to make sense of your notes.
- Make sure that you ask the teacher or check the material if there is anything that you do not understand.
- Don't forget that you can also create a mind map or diagram to record notes when listening as well as when reading.

Note taking from a DVD or computer program

Many of the same points mentioned above apply here. The advantage that you have of course is that you can pause and/or replay parts of the material that you need to hear again.

Activity

Your task is to look at the historiography of the causes of the Second World War in preparation for an essay: **Did Hitler cause the Second World War?**

Watch the following extract on YouTube and make notes.

Remember:

- try to distinguish between factual information and analysis
- do not include unnecessary information.

www.youtube.com/watch?v=FUngG2CRYdY&feature=related

Different styles of note taking

Notes need to be clear, useful and reflect your own style of learning. They must also be organized: you should aim for clear headings and subheadings; numbering of points; using colour, capitals and other forms of emphasis; and abbreviations (see page 16).

Activity

Below are students' notes on the question: **What was the impact of the First World War on Russia?**

Three different styles of note taking are shown. Each system contains basically the same information but it is laid out in a different way and with different levels of detail.

1 What abbreviations or techniques for emphasis have been used in each of the different systems?
2 How could you improve the content and layout of the notes in each of the systems?
3 What are the advantages and disadvantages of these different systems?

Tip

As you look at each note-taking method consider whether it:

- encourages you to be analytical as you write the notes; that is, think about connections and the importance of events
- includes enough detail (but discourages including too much irrelevant detail)
- shows the interconnections between events and ideas
- could be easily memorized
- could be easily added to.

Linear system

The impact of the First World War on Russia

Military

a **Events**

1914

After initial success, Russians defeated at Tannenberg and Masurian Lakes.

1915

Disastrous year; Germans capture Warsaw.

1916

Brusilov offensive. Russians made advances but not sustained.

b **Organization**

(i) Leadership inefficient – posts held through social standing rather than through merit. Soldiers poorly trained – conscript peasants.

(ii) Morale low due to lack of supplies and military failures.

Political

a **Role of Nicholas II, Tsarina and Rasputin**

(i) Tsar took over as commander in chief – therefore identified with failures and isolated from government.

(ii) Rasputin then had influence over appointments in government – led to constant changes.

(iii) Tsarina and Rasputin became discredited; alienated higher sections of society.

b Duma

    (i) Welcomed war in 1914.

    (ii) August 1915: expressed concern at handling of war. Set up 'Progressive Bloc' calling for a government of confidence – rejected by Tsar.

    (iii) 1916: challenged government again. Formed a committee which became the provisional government during the revolution.

Economic

a Industrial

    (i) Massive expansion of war production at expense of other industries.

    (ii) Production hit by supply problems of fuel and labour.

b Agriculture

    (i) Peasants kept grain back as value of money fell.

    (ii) Grain failed to reach cities – supply and transport problems.

c Financial

    (i) Government revenue fell (decline in exports, ban on sale of alcohol).

    (ii) Expenditure rose – so resorted to printing money.

    (iii) Rapid inflation – huge impact on workers.

NB: R Service – revolution not inevitable and happened because of 'the protracted, exhausting conflict of the First World War.'

Grid system

	Military	Political	Economic
1914	Tannenberg and Masurian Lakes – defeat	Duma welcomes war	War production increases – production in other areas decreases b/c no supplies/labour Gvt revenue falls – ban on alcohol/no exports
1915	Germans capture Warsaw	Tsar takes over as commander of army – identified with failures and isolated Rasputin left in charge Duma sets up 'Progressive Bloc'	Growing problems with supplies of food to cities
1916	Brusilov Offensive – initial success not sustained	R and Tsarina discredited – nobility alienated by R's appointments Duma challenges gvt. Sets up cttee which forms basis of PG	Gvt prints more money → inflation Cities lacking grain and fuel
1917		Higher levels of society alienated Revolution – PG takes over	Lack of food and fuel lead to demonstrations in Petrograd
General comments	Army poorly led – social status not on merit. Low morale due to lack of training and supplies and to defeats	*NB: R Service – revolution not inevitable and happened because of 'the protracted, exhausting conflict of the First World War'*	

Spider diagrams or mind maps

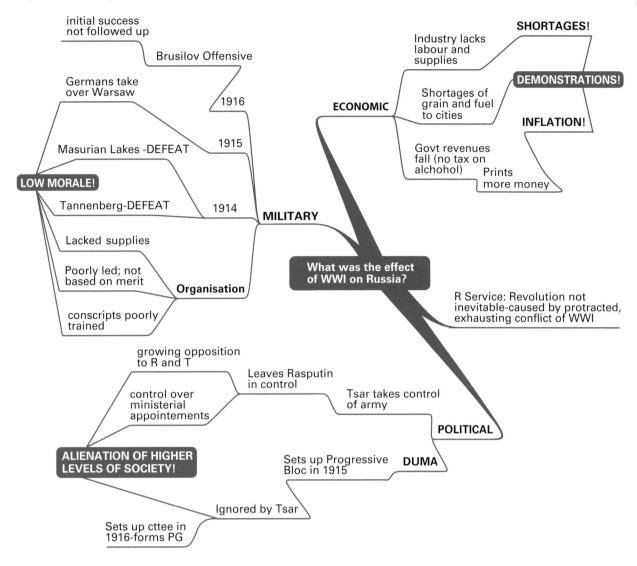

Some practical points:

- Be prepared with pen and paper as soon as you walk into the classroom – you don't want to miss key points while trying to find something to write on/with
- Always date your notes and make it clear the source they came from. Keep them in one place and in order
- Always be an 'active' note taker – looking for links, good quotes, thinking about questions or essay titles as you take the notes
- Leave space so you can add to your notes from other sources
- After a lesson, read up on what was discussed so that you can consolidate your class notes
- Review your notes periodically. This is the only way to really remember them
- Experiment with different methods

Activity

Put the same information shown in the spider diagram into a time line. What are the advantages and disadvantages of using a time line as your layout for note taking?

What other forms of note taking can you think of or do you use?

1914   1915   1916   1917   1918

Tip

Think about how you can convey information on a time line, for example using colour coding for different themes or putting certain information above the line and other information below the line.

Useful symbols and abbreviations to use when note taking

Symbols

→	leads to, produces, results in		∴	therefore
〉	greater than, more, larger		↑	increase
〈	less than, smaller, fewer than		↓	decrease
#	number		=	results in

Abbreviations

incl.	including		w/	with
excl.	excluding		w/o	without
re:	regarding, with reference to		b/c	because
approx.	approximately		s/t	something
ltd	limited		s/o	someone
vs	versus, against,		b/4,	before
v	very		govt.	government
vv	extremely		impt.	important
C	century			

Latin terms

N.B.   important note (from the Latin *nota bene:* mark well)

e.g.   for example (from the Latin *exempli gratia*)

i.e.   that is (from the Latin *id est*)

cf.   compare (from the Latin *confer*)

You can also develop your own abbreviations. For example, for different countries use the first letter of a country with a circle around it.

> **Activity**
>
> What is wrong with:
> - copying out lumps of solid text from books without changing anything?
> - substituting note taking from a textbook for highlighting only?
> - writing an essay straight from textbooks rather than making notes first?
> - long quotations?
> - notes without dates or data (such as statistics)?

Working with historical sources

As part of your research for essays – in particular your IA and extended essay – you will need to go beyond your textbook and use a range of historical sources. It is also important, however, that you examine these sources carefully to see how useful they are for your purpose.

To help you do this, always ask the following questions in order to assess the **origin** of the source.

- What type of source is it?
- Who produced it?
- What were the circumstances in which the source was produced? (This includes date, country, type of government, nature of censorship, etc.)

You then need to ask questions to identify the **purpose** of the source.

- What was the purpose or intention of the author?
- Who was intended to hear or read the source?

You also need to consider if there is evidence from other sources which supports the message of a particular source.

Every historical source needs to be looked at in relation to the questions above. However, it is possible to ask more specific questions about each type of source.

Below are five types of source that you will be using for your IA and extended essay investigations, with some suggestions of the type of questions that you should consider when using them. There will be more discussion about these sources, and also about primary sources, in chapter 2, which examines how to approach questions on evaluating sources in Paper 1.

Extracts from textbooks or works by historians

What is the purpose of the book? This question is relevant particularly when choosing to use textbooks or historians' work for your research. The aim of a textbook is to make information accessible to students and so will often be packaged clearly and succinctly. This has advantages for you as the reader as the information should be easy to digest. However, there is the possibility that particular information and/or analysis may be less detailed than work by a historian. For the IA and the extended essay in particular, it will be necessary to go beyond textbooks to look at books written by historians writing in the field in which you are interested in researching. (See page 8 on reading for information.)

When was the book published? This is important for giving an indication as to how up to date the textbook or historian's research is. New documents are released every year and so more recent books will have the advantage of access to more documents. For example, 1990 is a key date for books on the Soviet Union as this is the date after which historians had much greater access to Soviet archives.

What is the title of the book? From the title, you should be able to see what the purpose of the author is – whether it is to take a very broad view of an era or country or a very specific, in-depth look at a particular issue. This will affect the book's level of detail and therefore how useful it is to you.

Where was the book published and where does the author come from? This is relevant for censorship issues and access to documents.

Does the author have any personal interest in the topic he or she is writing about? Don't forget that most writers of textbooks and historians do attempt to be as impartial and professional as possible in their writing. For example, if a British person is writing about the role of Germany in causing the First World War, this will not automatically make the writer one-sided in his or her approach. If you suspect that the author has a particular purpose in his or her writing and is not taking a neutral approach, try to find evidence for this in the actual source.

How comprehensive is the bibliography and how rigorous is the referencing? Looking at the bibliography and checking the referencing will give you a good idea of the range of sources used and whether the writer's assertions are supported by evidence.

Consider the following source.

Using the points above, consider the value and limitations of this source for a student analysing the causes of the Cold War. Don't forget to research Gaddis's credentials as a Cold War historian.

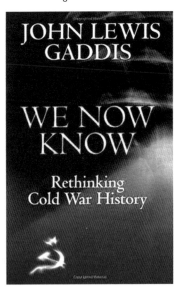

Gaddis, J. L., 1997, *We Now Know. Rethinking Cold War history,* New York: Oxford University Press.

John Lewis Gaddis

Biographies

Who is the author? Does the author have direct access to the subject or did he or she have to rely on accounts from others? Is the author likely to be someone who will give an objective account of his or her subject or someone who has an interest in putting the subject in a positive light?

Where was the book published and where does the author come from? Again, this is relevant for censorship issues and access to documents.

How comprehensive is the bibliography and how rigorous is the referencing? Looking at the bibliography and checking the referencing will give you a good idea of the range of sources used and whether the historian's assertions are supported by evidence.

Task 1

Find a biography of a key figure from the period of history you are studying. With reference to the questions above, analyse how useful you consider it would be in adding insight into your chosen period.

Chang, J. and Halliday, J., 2005, *Mao: The unknown story* Jonathan Cape: London.

Task 2

What questions would you ask about an autobiography in order to assess how useful it is for your research?

Internet sites

There many excellent online resources that you can now access as part of your research. However, you need to be just as rigorous in your analysis of these as you would be of written sources. Anybody can put up a web page and many sites are unregulated and not monitored, so it is essential to ask the following questions.

Who is the author of the website? As with evaluating the author of a history book, you need to consider the qualifications of the author and his or her likely experience and knowledge on the topic you are researching.

Is the author presenting the views for himself or herself? Or is the author writing under the umbrella of an organization such as a university or magazine (which therefore may well have approved the article).

When was the article posted?

Are there citations or a bibliography which would allow you to verify information given?

What is the purpose of the website? Is it a website designed specifically for students? If so, for students of what age? Will it cover your topic in enough depth? Is it a personal view on a topic (which could make it subjective)? Is it written for general interest – for historians as well as non-historians? Again, this might mean it lacks specific detail.

Activity

Consider the following websites:

www.bbc.co.uk/history/worldwars/wwone/

www.wilsoncenter.org/index.cfm?fuseaction=topics.home&topic_id=1409

www.spartacus.schoolnet.co.uk

Using the points above, consider the value and limitations of using these sites for historical research for your IA or extended essay.

Documentary film

What is the title of the documentary? Is it likely to present a broad overview of the topic or to look at one aspect of the topic in depth?

What is the purpose of the documentary? Is it aiming to appeal to a broad adult audience or is it designed for schools? Is it aiming to be 'sensational'; that is, to reveal new information or a new interpretation of events for the first time? If so, what evidence is presented to support this? Are reputable historians interviewed in the documentary to support the claims put forward?

What is the style of the documentary? This is linked to its purpose. Many documentaries are made in a 'docu-drama' style to make them more interesting; does that affect their factual content?

When was the documentary made? Is it likely to include up-to-date evidence?

What reviews are there of the documentary? Did it generate any controversy?

Activity

Research the following historical documentaries (you can see excerpts on YouTube and read reviews on the Internet).

- CNN Cold War documentary
- 'The First World War': documentary series to accompany Hew Strachan's book on the First World War
- The Kennedys – docu-drama, 2011

What are the value and limitations of these documentaries for IB historical research?

Historical vocabulary

Increasing your historical vocabulary is important to help you in your reading and to increase your understanding.

Below are (only some) key historical terms that you should know the meaning of. Find out the meanings of any of the words you don't know.

Write them down in your own glossary. You can then add new words to your glossary as you come across them in your reading.

anarchy	civil war	imperialism	radical
blockade	democracy	liberalism	reactionary
bourgeoisie	dictator	limited war	republic
capitalist	fascism	nationalism	revolution
conservative	franchise	proletariat	sanctions
coup d'état	guerrilla warfare	propaganda	socialism

Working with sources

When you work with sources you are practising a key component of a historian's methodology. Paper 1 skills are the skills that historians apply when they are researching a historical question and attempting to reach a conclusion.

In Paper 1 you will:

- **interpret and analyse** information from a variety of sources
- **compare and contrast** information between sources
- **evaluate** sources for their value and limitations
- **synthesize** evidence from the sources with your own detailed knowledge of the topic.

> 'As historians, our training and discipline is based on documentary evidence'
>
> DAVID DIXON

Activity

Read the following comment on sources and then answer the questions that follow.

> The practice of history begins with evidence and with sources. The availability of sources is often the key determinant of what becomes popular, because some areas, for example nineteenth century France, benefit from greater volume of documents than others, such as ancient Germany. Whereas historians of early modern political history face a veritable forest of official documents – more than any one person could marshal in a lifetime. It is vital, therefore, that students of history be aware of the scope of historical sources, and the methods which historians use to order them.
>
> Black, J., and Macraild, D. M., 2007, *Studying History*, Palgrave Study Skills, Basingstoke: Palgrave Macmillan, third edn., pg. 89.

- According to Black and Macraild, what makes certain historical subjects more popular than others?
- What problem do contemporary historians face?

What can you expect on Paper 1?

Paper 1 has a key advantage of being somewhat **predictable**. You can predict the nature and style of the four questions on this paper. This means that you can also learn and practise the correct approach for each of these questions and maximize the marks you attain **technically**.

The prescribed subjects

You will study one of three prescribed in-depth subjects for Paper 1. As it is a 'prescribed' subject you will need to ensure you have learned each sub-topic from the bullet point list set down in the syllabus. In addition, you are expected to have some background knowledge in order to put the study into its historical context.

After you have studied one of the prescribed subjects, you should be able to demonstrate knowledge and understanding of the key historical terms and concepts associated with your topic, for example:

'isolationism' and 'collective security' (prescribed subject 1)
'Arabism' and 'Zionism' (prescribed subject 2)
'power struggle' and 'perestroika' (prescribed subject 3).

You should show an awareness of different approaches to and interpretations of historical events related to the prescribed subject. It is also important for you to practise using both primary (contemporary) and secondary sources on the topic you are studying for Paper 1, as well as regularly practising the different styles of question set on this paper.

In summary: you should be able to 'critically engage with a range of historical sources related to the prescribed subject in order to comprehend, analyse and evaluate them in a historical context'. *IB Diploma Programme History guide*, March 2008, pg. 14.

The examination

Although you will know which prescribed subject you are being examined on before you enter the examination room, you will not know which of the bullets or themes the paper will specifically focus on. Don't worry if you are not familiar with some of the documents, or people or even certain events, mentioned in the sources; your contextual knowledge and document skills will allow you to answer the questions.

You will be given five sources. There will be a statement above the sources that explains the theme of the paper and sources, for example as follows.

Prescribed subjects: May 2010

Prescribed subject 1
These sources and questions relate to the Abyssinian Crisis (1935–36).

Prescribed subject 2
These sources and questions relate to the United Nations Partition Plan, the outbreak of the civil war (1947–1948) and its results.

Prescribed subject 3
These sources and questions relate to China under Deng Xiaoping: political changes, and their limits, culminating in Tiananmen Square (1989).

The focus for each of these sentences will be taken directly from bullet points in the guide and you should highlight the sentence and use it to guide your initial reading of the paper.

The sources on the paper will be a selection of both primary and secondary sources. The length of each source may vary – but generally it will be around 750 words long. Usually **one** of the five sources will be a more 'visual' rather than text-based source, for example a photograph, cartoon, table of statistics or graph.

Use your 5 minutes of reading time to note and understand how the sources are related to the **theme** of the paper. Read through the questions and begin to read through the first sources. Reading the questions during this time will help you to understand what to focus on when you read the sources thoroughly. Do not ignore the italicized introduction for each source as this often contains important contextual information.

Second-language students are allowed to take a translation dictionary into the examination. Remember that this is not a test of your language skills and more difficult words are usually explained in brackets within the document.

It is **not** a vocabulary test, but it is an assessment of your historical understanding. Remember that a phrase may mean something different in a certain historical context, and that the 'tone' of a speech, for example, might only be understood within its historical context.

How do I best use my time?

Timing is a key issue for students in paper 1 as often you can run out of time before finishing the last question. This is significant as the final question carries the most marks: 8 of the 25 total. To prepare properly for this paper you must practise past Paper 1 examples in full and under timed conditions.

One suggestion for how you might break down your time is:

6 minutes	read through and highlight documents
10 minutes	answer question 1 parts a and b
12 minutes	answer question 2
12 minutes	answer question 3
20 minutes	answer question 4.

Other teachers and examiners have suggested incorporating the reading time for documents into the response time for each question:

10 minutes	read relevant documents and answer question 1 parts a and b
15 minutes	read relevant documents and answer question 2
15 minutes	read relevant documents and answer question 3
20 minutes	read relevant documents and **plan** and answer question 4.

You will have to decide which method works best for you. Either way, it is strongly recommended that you aim to have 20 minutes at the end of the examination for question 4, which is the mini-essay question.

The questions

The questions will ask you to apply the various techniques of document analysis and evaluation to the given sources – which may well be documents that you have not have seen before.

Question 1

This is in two parts. It is made up of a 2-mark and 3-mark component – giving you a total of 5 possible marks. It is assessing your **historical comprehension** of the sources. You do not need to give your own knowledge in your response.

This is the only question that asks you to explain **what** the documents say. The other questions require you to **use** the information.

Part a

The 3-mark question asks you to comprehend, extract and possibly infer information. Here are some suggestions for answering this question.

- Write: firstly…, secondly…, thirdly… to ensure that you make at least three separate points.
- Do not make the same point more than once.
- Do not overly rely on quotation – make your point and then briefly quote two or three words of the source.

Part b

- You should try to make two clear points for this question.

- Establish the overall message or point made in the source, and then refer to the content of the source to elaborate and further explain its message.

For question 1 parts a and b you should not need to bring in your own knowledge; however, we would hope that your contextual understanding of the topic and sources will enable you to understand the message of the sources more clearly.

Activity

Below are two different types of part a question and two different types of part b question. Read the sample answers and decide how many marks you would give each answer. Then read the examiner's comments.

Remember that for this question you must make at least three valid points to gain 3 marks, two valid points for 2 marks and so on.

Question 1 part a (May 2010)

Prescribed subject 1

Source A

Extract from the *Covenant of the League of Nations*, 1919.

Article 16 – Should any member of the League resort to war in disregard of its covenants under Articles 12, 13 or 15, it shall be deemed to have committed an act of war against all other members of the League, which hereby undertake immediately to subject it to the severance [cutting off] of all trade or financial relations, the prohibition of all exchange between their nationals and the nationals of the covenant-breaking state, and the prevention of all financial, commercial or personal business between the nationals of the covenant-breaking state and the nationals of any other state, whether a member of the League or not.

It shall be the duty of the Council in such cases to recommend to the several governments concerned what effective military, naval or air force the members of the League shall contribute to the armed forces to be used to protect the covenants of the League.

What, according to source A, was the significance of Article 16 of the *Covenant of the League of Nations?* [3 marks]

© IB Organization 2010

Sample answer

The significance of Article 16 of the Covenant was that, firstly, it made it clear that if any member resorted to war it would be considered to have made an 'act of war' against all other members. Secondly, it specified that this act of war would lead to the 'severance' of all trade relations and, thirdly, that the Council would then recommend to the governments concerned the military forces each member had to contribute to protect the League.

Your mark:

Your comment:

Examiner's comment

This answer would score 3 marks as it clearly has three points on the significance of Article 16.

Prescribed subject 2 (May 2010)

Source A

United Nations General Assembly (UNGA) Partition Plan, 29 November 1947 (UN Resolution 181). Reprinted with permission.

What does source A suggest about the United Nations Partition Plan of 1947? [3 marks]

© IB Organization 2010

Sample answer

The source suggests that Palestine has been divided into two areas – one area for the Jews and one for the Palestinians with Jerusalem being an international zone. However, the division involves a rather unequal distribution with Jews gaining more land by the sea, for example Jaffa – the biggest port. The Arab land is also split into three different areas which would make crossing between the different areas difficult.

Your mark:

Your comment:

Examiner's comment

This answer would score 2 marks as only two clear points have been made.

Question 1 part b

Prescribed subject 1

Source A

A cartoon by David Low, published in the *Star* newspaper, 5 September 1922.

"Young Feller, the report has been greatly exaggerated."

What is the cartoonist's message about the League of Nations in the early 1920s?

[2 marks]

© IB Organization 2010

Sample answer A
The cartoonist shows a small boy carrying a coffin labelled 'war'. A fierce looking adult man warns him that the war is not yet 'over.'

Your mark:

Your comment:

Examiner's comment
No valid points are made regarding the message of the cartoon – there is only a description of the cartoon.

Sample answer B
The message of the cartoonist was that the League of Nations had weaknesses from the outset and that it might not be able to prevent future wars. The League is holding a heavy casket or coffin which might symbolize the League's inability to act quickly to prevent conflict. The League itself is young and not strong or experienced in this cartoon which might be an allusion to the absence of key strong powers like the United States; opponents to peace, the 'God of War' here, is shown as being strong and not intimidated by the presence of the League.

Your mark:

Your comment:

Examiner's comment
The message of the cartoon is clearly stated at the beginning of the answer. The details of the cartoon are then given in order to explain this message more clearly. There are more than two valid points given here.

Note that you can also have 2-mark questions that ask you to explain the message in a photograph, or in a painting, or of a speech or other written text.

Prescribed subject 2

Source B

Schulze, K. E., 2008, *The Arab-Israeli Conflict,* Harlow: Pearson Education.

… While Zionist politicians did not like the status of Jerusalem, they accepted the UN plan as a first step to statehood. The Arabs were outraged. They could not find any redeeming aspect in a plan that allotted part of their territory to the Zionists… Immediately following the general assembly vote, both Arabs and Jews started to arm themselves. What ensued was a civil war between Jews and Palestinian Arabs, all within Palestine. The months before the end of the mandate were characterized by bitter fighting – including the massacre at the Arab village of Deir Yassin by the Irgun and Lehi which killed 250, the Arab ambush on a Jewish medical convoy killing 75, and the Arab siege of Jerusalem – ultimately resulting in a mass exodus of Palestinian Arabs. By May 1948, when the

British finally withdrew, over 300,000 Arabs had fled from what was to become the new Jewish state… Historians have argued about the causes of this flight ever since.

According to source B, what were the reactions to the United Nations Partition Plan? [2 marks]

Your mark:

Your comment:

Examiner's comment
This has two clear points and would get 2 marks.

Sample answer
One reaction to the Partition Plan was that it was rejected by the Arabs who were unwilling to have any of their land given to the Jews. Another reaction is that both sides started to arm themselves.

Activity

Choose the prescribed subject that you are studying from the questions below. Answer the question and check your response against the mark schemes that follow.

Prescribed subject 1

Source A

From an article on the results of the Disarmament Conference, published in *Izvestia* newspaper, 26 July 1932. (*Izvestia* was the official newspaper of the Soviet government.)

After five years of preparation and six months of work, the labours of the Disarmament Conference have come to an end, having accomplished nothing… what then did the Geneva conference do in the course of six months? All the capitalist countries presented declarations disguised in pacifist phrases which defended their specific programmes of rearmament. The French in particular refused to agree to any limitations on armaments… French imperialism refused to agree to any limitation on armaments and proposed instead to place the most powerful instruments of warfare into the hands of a special army controlled by the League of Nations. The French proposal did not aim at the limitation of armaments, but rather at the legalization by the League of Nations of all instruments of warfare…

Only the Soviet Union presented a clear and exact programme of disarmament, pointing out that disarmament alone will safeguard the people of the world from the unheard calamities of modern warfare… this proposal was rejected by all of the capitalist countries.

Source B

A cartoon by David Low, 'The Conference excuses itself', published in the *Evening Standard* newspaper, 23 May 1934.

1 **a** Identify the key points made by *Izvestia* in source A on why the disarmament conference failed. [3 marks]

 b What is the message conveyed by the cartoonist in source B? [2 marks]

Mark scheme

Part a

Your answer should include at least three of the following points.

- Capitalist countries only 'presented' pacifist declarations while they were really defending their own rearmament programmes.
- The French were particularly responsible for the failure as they refused any limitations.
- The French proposal aimed to legalize by the League of Nations all instruments of warfare.
- The USSR was the only country to present a clear programme of disarmament, which was rejected by the capitalist states.

Go through the source and highlight all these points.

Part b

Your answer should include the **overall message** of the cartoon and then an explanation of how this message is delivered.

- The cartoonist is critical of the leaders, governments and statesmen who failed to agree on a programme of disarmament.
- The leaders are represented by carnivorous animals – which could be associated with aggression and war.
- The 'people' of the world are passive, non-aggressive sheep who are being blamed for the failures of their leaders to work for peace.

Annotate the cartoon to highlight the three points made in the mark scheme.

Prescribed subject 2

Source A

Article 17 from the *Covenant of the PLO,* 28 May 1964.

The partitioning of Palestine in 1947 and the establishment of Israel are illegal and false regardless of the loss of time, because they were contrary to the wish of the Palestine people and its natural right to its homeland, and in violation of the basic principles embodied in the charter of the United Nations, foremost among which is the right to self determination.

Source B

A cartoon by William Papas, published in the *Guardian* newspaper, 5 June 1967.

1 a Identify the key points made in source A regarding the partition of Palestine in 1947. [3 marks]

b What is the message conveyed by the cartoonist in source B? [2 marks]

Mark scheme

Part a

Your answer should include at least three of the following points.

- The partition and establishment of Israel is illegal.
- The partition is against the wishes of the Palestinian people.
- The Palestinian people have a natural right to their homeland.
- The partition is against the basic principles embodied in the UN charter.
- The key principle violated is the right to self determination.

Go through the source and highlight all these points.

Mark scheme

Part b

Your answer should include the overall message of the cartoon and then an explanation of how this message is delivered.

- The cartoonist is critical of the Egyptian and Israeli leaders for shutting out the UN.
- The leaders are both heavily armed.
- The leaders are 'guarding' a locked prison-style door, keeping the UN's involvement out.
- There is a stalemate or deadlock between them.
- There is nothing preventing a fight between them.

Annotate the cartoon to highlight the all points made in the mark scheme.

Prescribed subject 3

Source A

US President Carter's address to US Congress, 8 January 1980.

The Soviet invasion of Afghanistan is the greatest threat to peace since the Second World War. It's a sharp escalation in the aggressive history of the Soviet Union. We are the other superpower on earth, and it became my responsibility to take action. Our own nation's security was directly threatened. There is no doubt that the Soviet's move into Afghanistan, if done without adverse consequences, would have resulted in the temptation to move again and again until they reached warm water ports or until they acquired control over a major portion of the world's oil supplies.

Source B

A cartoon published in Britain, 4 January 1980. (The figures represent members of the British government including Margaret Thatcher who was prime minister at the time.)

www.cartoons.ac.uk/record/33759

1 a According to source A, what were the United States' reasons for its strong reaction to the Soviet invasion of Afghanistan? [3 marks]

b What is the message of the cartoonist in source B concerning the Soviet invasion of Afghanistan? [2 marks]

Mark scheme

Part a

Your answer should include at least three of the following points.

- Soviet invasion was the greatest threat to peace since the Second World War.
- It was an escalation in Soviet aggression and the United States had the responsibility to take action.
- US security was threatened.
- If the United States had not responded this would have encouraged the USSR to carry out further acts of aggression and expansion, for example to gain warm water ports or to control oil supplies.

Go through the source and highlight all these points.

Mark scheme

Part b

Your answer should include the overall message of the cartoon and then an explanation of how this message is delivered.

- The cartoonist is critical of the Soviet invasion, but also critical of the British government's passive and unprepared response.
- The Soviets are depicted as an 'escaped' bear – which had broken free of its cage and was dangerous.
- British government leaders are represented as scared, and shocked at finding the 'bear' has broken free.
- The cartoon gives the idea of the Soviet Union now being 'unleashed' through its invasion.

Annotate the cartoon to highlight all these points.

Question 2

Question 2 will ask you to **compare** and **contrast** two documents. Your aim is to identify similar themes and ideas in two sources and also to identify differences between them. Question 2 is marked out of a total of 6 marks.

The key to this question is **linkage**; that is, you are expected to discuss the sources together throughout your response. The examiner is looking for a **running commentary**. At no time should you talk about one source without relating it to the other. 'End-on accounts' – where you write about the content of one source followed by the content of the second source – do not score well.

Note that the mark scheme for IB examiners includes the following:

'End-on description of the sources would probably be worth 3 marks if the comparative element is only implicit, and 4 marks with explicit linkage. If the linkage is excellent or detailed material is presented in a comparative framework, 5 or 6 marks could be scored'.

How to approach question 2

You must find **both** similarities and differences. This is best presented as two separate paragraphs – one for comparisons and one for contrasts.

- Using two highlighter pens highlight the similarities in each source in one colour and the differences in another colour. This will make it easier for your to write your answer.
- Always be clear about which source you are discussing.

- Find the more obvious similarities and differences and then go on to identify more specific comparisons and contrasts.
- Deal with similarities in your first paragraph and differences in your second.
- For each point that you make, briefly quote from the sources (only two or three words) to support that point.
- Don't write an introduction to your answer or attempt a conclusion. This is not necessary and wastes time.
- Don't waste time explaining what the sources say.

Examiner's hint

Note that you must make more than **one** comparison and more than **one** contrast to achieve the maximum marks in a compare and contrast question.

How to draw comparisons and show similarities	**How to draw contrasts and show differences**
Both source A and source B…	Source A suggests… . However, source B says…
Source A suggests… . Similarly, source B suggests…	Source B disagrees with source A regarding…
Source A supports source B…	Source A claims… , as opposed to source B which asserts…
Like source B, source A says…	Source B goes further than source A in arguing…
In the same way that source B argues… , source A points out that…	Source A highlights… , but source B does not mention this.

Examiner's hint

What *not* to do!

The focus of this question is **how** the sources are similar or different and is asking you to look at the content of the source. This question is **not** asking you about **why** the sources might be similar or different which would then ask you to consider the origin and purpose of the sources.

Don't use grids, charts or bullet points – always write in full paragraphs.

Activity

Below are two sample answers to an example question 2. Read the sample answers and decide how many marks you would give each answer. Then read the examiner's comment.

Also go through each answer and highlight the 'linking' vocabulary that each answer has used when comparing and contrasting the sources.

Prescribed subject 1

Compare and contrast the views in source A and source B (below) on the Treaty of Versailles.

Source A

Nicolson, H., 1965, *Peacemaking*, New York: Grosset & Dunlap (first published 1933).

The historian, with every justification, will come to the conclusion that we were very stupid men. I think we were… We came to Paris confident that the new world order was about to be established; we left it convinced the new order had fouled the old… We arrived determined that a peace of justice and wisdom should be negotiated: we left it conscious that the treaties imposed were neither just nor wise… It is impossible to read German criticism without deriving the impression that the Paris Peace Conference was guilty of disguising an imperialist peace under the surface of Wilsonism… Hypocrisy was the predominant and inescapable result… We had accepted a system for others which, when it came to practice we should refuse to apply to ourselves.

Sample answer

Source A and source B agree that Germany had been badly treated in the treaty. Source A suggests that historians will view the peacemakers as 'stupid men' and source B says that they have reduced a generation of Germans to servitude. Source B differs from source A as it focuses on specific provisions whereas source A simply looks at the 'big picture'.

Your mark:

Your comment:

Examiner's comment

This question has the right structure and the student seems to understand how to approach the question. However, this would not score more than 2 marks out of 6 as it does not develop the comparisons in enough detail. Similarly, the second paragraph is too vague. The student needs to provide much more specific contrasts.

Prescribed subject 3

Compare and contrast the views expressed in sources A and C on the reasons for the Soviet involvement in Afghanistan.   [6 marks]

Source A

Carter's address to the US Congress, 8 January 1980.

The Soviet invasion of Afghanistan is the greatest threat to peace since the Second World War. It's a sharp escalation in the aggressive history of the Soviet Union. We are the other superpower on earth, and it became my responsibility to take action. Our own nation's security was directly threatened. There is no doubt that the Soviet's move into Afghanistan, if done without adverse consequences, would have resulted in the temptation to move again and again until they reached warm water ports or until they acquired control over a major portion of the world's oil supplies.

Source C

Brezhnev's announcement at the 26th Party Congress, February 1981.

Imperialism launched the present undeclared war against the Afghan revolution. That created a direct threat and a danger to our southern border. The situation compelled us to provide the armed assistance this friendly country was asking for… As far as the Soviet military contingent is concerned, we will be prepared to withdraw it with the concurrence of the Afghan government. For this to happen, the infiltration of counterrevolutionary bands into Afghanistan must be completely stopped. This must be formalized in accords between Afghanistan and its neighbors. Dependable guarantees that there will be no new intervention are needed. This is the principled position of the Soviet Union, and we will firmly adhere to it! (Applause.)

Sample answer

The sources are similar in that they both indicate that the Soviets have a military presence in Afghanistan. Source A refers to an invasion whereas source C talks of 'armed assistance'. Both sources also imply that the situation is a serious one that needs addressing; Carter in source A calls the situation 'the greatest threat to peace since the Second World War' and Brezhnev uses the words 'threat' and 'danger' in describing the situation.

However, these sources contrast significantly on the reasons for the Soviet involvement in Afghanistan. Source A says that the reason for Soviet intervention is because of an 'escalation' in Soviet 'aggression' whereas Brezhnev in source C says that the Soviets are there not because of any aggression but because they were asked to provide 'assistance' by a 'friendly' country. Brezhnev further says that they are there for security reasons. However, the United States sees it as the first step in the USSR's attempt to gain 'control over a major portion of the world's oil supplies'. Brezhnev also implies that Western 'imperialism' created the situation which required the USSR to go into Afghanistan whereas this fact is ignored in source A.

Your mark:

Your comment:

Examiner's comment

The student here has clearly addressed both similarities and differences. There is very good linkage with appropriate quotes from each source to back up the points made. The answer would have scored 6 marks.

Activity

Read the sources below and then try writing an answer to the example question 2 that follows.

Before starting on the question, take two different coloured highlighter pens and highlight the **similarities** in the comments in the sources in one colour and the **differences** between them in another.

Check your answer against the mark scheme.

Source C

Speech broadcast to the German nation by Adolf Hitler, 14 October 1933.

Germany cannot tolerate the deliberate degradation of the nation by the perpetuation of a discrimination which consists in withholding the rights which are granted as a matter of course to other nations… The men who are at present the leaders of Germany have nothing in common with the traitors of November 1918. Like every decent English man and every decent French man, we have all had our duty to our Fatherland and placed our lives at its service. We are not responsible for the war, but we feel responsible for what every honest man must do in the time of his country's distress and for what we have done. We have such infinite love for our people that we desire whole-heartedly an understanding with other nations… but, as men of honour, it is impossible for us to be members of institutions under conditions which are only bearable to those who have no sense of honour… Since it has been made clear to us from the declarations of certain great powers that they were not prepared to consider real equality of rights for us at present, we have decided that it is impossible, in the view of the indignity of her position, for Germany to continue to force her company upon other nations.

Source E

McDonough, F., 2002, *Hitler, Chamberlain and Appeasement*, Cambridge University Press, pg. 1.

The first major intervention into foreign affairs by Hitler was his decision in October 1933 to withdraw Germany simultaneously from the League of Nations and the much-hyped World Disarmament Conference. These decisions were very strongly supported inside Nazi Germany. Withdrawal from the League of Nations allowed Germany to act as a free agent in European affairs, while leaving the Disarmament Conference gave the German army the opportunity to push ahead with rearmament.

Hitler claimed that Germany was being refused equal treatment by the League of Nations and was also being prevented from rearming by the intransigence of the French government, which, he claimed, desired to keep the German armed forces in a permanent state of inferiority. Ramsey MacDonald, the British prime minister, interpreted Hitler's desire to rearm in a spirit of trust and understanding, and viewed French obsession with security as the main obstacle to a disarmament agreement. It was, of course, very difficult for the French government to accept that a German regime, led by such an extreme German nationalist as Hitler, should be granted the right to expand its armed forces with complete freedom.'

Compare and contrast the views expressed in sources C and E on why Germany left the Disarmament Conference and the League of Nations. [6 marks]

Check your comparisons and contrasts against the possible responses below.

Comparisons include comments about:

- the influence and policies of France
- French attempts to limit Germany's armed forces
- the unpopularity of the disarmament conference in Germany.

Contrasts include comments about:

- the role of Britain (source C)
- how Hitler wanted to act freely and be unrestrained (source E)
- indignity (source C).

Question 3

As you have read in chapter 1, historians need to use and evaluate sources as they research a historical era or event. For question 3, you need to evaluate different sources in terms of their 'value' and 'limitations' by examining their origin and purpose.

To find the origin and purpose of a source look carefully at the information that introduces it and pose the following questions.

For origin	For purpose
Who wrote it, said it, drew it, etc.?	**Why** did they write it, say it, draw it?
When did they write it, say it, draw it?	**Who** did they write it, say it, draw it **for**?
Where did they write it, say it, draw it?	
What is the source – a speech, cartoon, textbook, etc.?	

From the information you have on the origins of each source, and what you can infer about the document's purpose, you must explain the value and limitations each source has for historians researching a particular event or period in history.

The grid below gives you an idea of the kinds of values and limitations connected with different primary sources. For a review of the issues connected to secondary sources, refer back to pages 16–20.

Examiner's comment

Note that value and limitations given here are general or 'generic' points that could be applied to these sources. However, your contextual knowledge and the specific provenance of any source that you get in the examination will allow you to make much more specific comments on the value and limitations of the source that you evaluate in a document question. Notice also that how valuable the source is always depends on what you are using it for.

Source	Values	Limitations
Private letters (audience is the recipient) Diaries (the audience is personal not public at the time of writing)	Can offer insight into **personal** views or opinions Can indicate effects of an event or era on an individual Can suggest motives for public actions and opinions	Only gives individual opinion, not a general view or government perspective Writer may change opinion due to later events, may give a view not held in public Motive might be to persuade audience (in the case of a letter) to act in certain way
Memoirs (to be published for a public audience)	Can offer insight into **personal** views, suggest motives for public actions and might benefit from hindsight – an evaluation of events after the period Might show how the individual **wants** his or her motive and actions to be viewed by the public	Writer may revise opinions with the benefit of hindsight (that is, now the consequences of actions are known) Writer might want to highlight the strengths of his or her actions – to improve his or her public image or legacy
Newspapers, television and radio reports, eyewitness accounts	Can give **publicly** held views or popular opinion Might offer an **expert's** view Can give insight into **contemporary** opinion	Could be politically influenced or could be censored by specific governments or regimes Might only give an overview of the situation Might only give a one-sided, narrow perspective Might emphasize only a minor part of an issue (Note that eyewitnesses are not useful just because they are at an event; each eyewitness will notice different aspects and may miss key points altogether)
Novels, poems	Could **inform** contemporary opinion Might offer **insight** into emotional responses and motive	Could be a 'dissenting' voice (that is, not popular opinion) Could exaggerate the importance of an event or individual Could have a political agenda
Statistics	Can offer insights e.g. into economic growth and decline Might suggest **correlations** between indicators, for example unemployment and voting patterns Makes analysis of results over time easier Make **comparisons** easier	The purpose of gathering particular statistics needs considering – could be political, economic or deliberately distorted Could relate only to one location or time period Correlations might be wrong – there could be another causal factor not included in the statistics
Photographs	Can give sense of **a specific scene** or event Can offer insight into immediate response to or impact of an event on particular people or a place Might offer information on the environment	Cannot see beyond the 'lens' The limited view might distort the 'bigger' picture Might be staged The purpose of the photographer is key; what did he or she want to show?
Cartoons and paintings	Can **inform** public opinion – cartoonists often respond to commonly held views When governments or regimes censor the press, can be used to portray the **government's** line	Could be censored so not public opinion Cartoons often play on stereotypes and exaggeration Could be limited to the viewpoint and experience of cartoonist or artist (or the newspaper or periodical the artwork appears in)

Government records and documents, speeches, memoranda	Might show the government's position or stance on an issue Can offer insight into reasons for decisions Might reveal **motives** for policies Can show what the public is told about an event or issue by government Might be a well-informed analysis	Often do not offer insight into results of policies and decisions Might not reveal dissent or divergent opinion Might not show public opinion Very sensitive information can be classified for many years May not explain motives for a decision or political purpose
Historians (see also page 17)	Are usually professionals, **experts** in the field Have the benefit of hindsight which contemporary sources do not May have access to a variety of documents, when relevant classified documents become available	Might have a broad focus to their work or might have a very specific and narrow focus Might be expert in another region or era May be influenced by their experience, politics or context

Activity

Below is a table with a variety of different sources in the first column. Try to fill in the blank columns – establishing what **type** of source each example is, and some basic ideas about the source's potential **values** and **limitations** from its **origin and purpose**. Note that this activity is just a starting point, as when you evaluate your sources on Paper 1 you will be able to add depth to your evaluation, based on your knowledge of the **context** of the documents you are given.

Source	Type of source	Values	Limitations
Hsu, I., 2000, *The Rise of Modern China*, New York: Oxford University Press. One cannot question the right of any government to defend itself when threatened with the danger of extinction. The question here, however, was not survival or extinction but meeting with student leaders to discuss anti-corruption measures and political liberalization. Essentially, the issue was whether the government judged the challenge correctly and honestly and devised counter-measures appropriate to the occasion. The answer must be 'no'. The threat to the Chinese leadership in May–June 1989 was largely fabricated, ultimately giving the government an excuse to kill the peaceful demonstrators as 'anti-party counter-revolutionaries'.			
Keynes, J. M., 1919, *The Economic Consequences of Peace*, New York: Harcourt, Brace and Howe. Keynes was an economist and high-ranking official in the British delegation of the Paris Peace Conference. … The policy of reducing Germany to servitude for a generation, of degrading the lives of millions of human beings, and of depriving a whole nation of happiness, should be abhorrent and detestable… Nations are not authorised, by religion or by natural morals, to visit on the children of their enemies the misdoings of parents or of rulers…			
Cartoon published in the *Daily Telegraph* newspaper, 24 May 1967. "*If Israel wants to threaten us with war, they are welcome.*"			

A German photograph of French troops in the Ruhr in 1923.

Almanac. 26 State Statistical Bureau, 23 February 1988, *Beijing Review*, March 7–13, 1988, Hsu, fifth edn., pg. 857.

Output of major industries	1965	1978	1981	1984	1987
Coal (100 million tons)	2.36	6.18	6.22	7.89	9.20
Crude oil (million tons)	11.31	104.05	101.22	114.61	134.00
Natural gas (100 million cubic metres)	11.00	137.30	127.40	124.30	140.15
Electricity (billion kwh)	67.6	256.6	309.3	377.0	496.0
Steel (million tons)	12.23	31.78	35.60	43.47	56.02

Extract from the poem 'Pantoum of the Great Depression', by the US poet Donald Justice.

At no time did anyone say anything in verse.
It was the ordinary pities and fears consumed us,
And if we suffered we kept quiet about it.
No audience would ever know our story.

It was the ordinary pities and fears consumed us.
We gathered on porches; the moon rose; we were poor.
What audience would ever know our story?
Beyond our windows shone the actual world.

We gathered on porches; the moon rose; we were poor.
And time went by, drawn by slow horses.
Somewhere beyond our windows shone the actual world.
The Great Depression had entered our souls like fog.

Moshe Dayan, Defence minister of Israel, interviewed for CBS 'Face the Nation' – a US television programme – in New York, June 1967.

Interviewer: 'Is there any possible way that Israel could absorb the huge numbers of Arabs whose territory it has gained control of now?'
Dayan: 'Economically we can; but I think that is not in accord with our aims in the future… we want to have a Jewish State. We can absorb them, but then it won't be the same country.'
Interviewer: 'And it is necessary to maintain this as a Jewish State and purely a Jewish State?'
Dayan: 'Absolutely – absolutely. We want a Jewish State like the French have a French State.' [p.xx   ]

Extract from letter from the British High Commissioner in Egypt, Sir Henry McMahon, to the Sherif of Mecca, Ali Ibn Husain, 1915. From *Great Britain Parliamentary Papers*, 1939, Misc. No. 3, Cmd. 5957. …I am empowered in the name of the Government of Great Britain to give the following assurances and make the following reply to your letter: (1) Subject to the above modifications, Great Britain is prepared to recognise and support the independence of the Arabs in all the regions within the limits demanded by the Sherif of Mecca. (2) Great Britain will guarantee the Holy Places against all external aggression and will recognise their inviolability…			
Edited version of an account published by the Palestinian Liberation Organization's Research Centre in Beirut, Lebanon, in 1972. 'My name is Ghazi Daniel and I am 24 years old. I was born in Nazareth but today I am stateless. In May 1948 when I was nine months old my family was forced to leave our beloved land. Father who was working in Haifa had to leave his job and mother who was managing a shop we owned had to close it. Our house in Nazareth became deserted and our land, tilled by my uncles, was seized. We became destitute refugees in Lebanon… Unlike the childhood of others, mine was full of sad memories. A few months after our arrival we were penniless and had to move into a refugee camp with 2,000 other homeless Palestinians. It is beyond human endurance for a family of eleven to live in a small tent through all the seasons of the year on UNRWA rations. Fathers buried their children… some buried their fathers…. [p.xx]			

Activity

Now choose a topic you have studied in your IB Diploma Programme history course. In pairs, find examples of each of the above types of source. With reference to their origin and purpose, discuss the values and limitations of each for studying your topic.

Examiner's hint

Note that for the purposes of evaluation, a source is not more or less useful just because it is primary or secondary. Always focus on the specific origins and purpose of a source – not whether it is primary or secondary. You do not need to give this distinction in your answer.

Activity

Read the extract below then answer the question that follows.

N.B. Disraeli was a 19-century British Conservative Party leader, and British prime minister from 1874–1880.

> Part of the problem for historians is defining what is a source. Although primary sources are usually closest, or indeed contemporary, to the period under observation, and secondary sources those works written subsequently, the distinction is actually quite blurred. Once we move away from simple cases (like politicians' diaries or cabinet minutes) which are clearly primary, difficulties do arise. Take Benjamin Disraeli's novel of 1845, *Sybil; or the Two Nations*. This is first and foremost a piece of fiction… For historians… however, *Sybil* is something of a primary source: it typifies the milieu (social setting) of the young Tory Radicals of the day (of whom Disraeli was one)…
>
> Black, J., and Macraild, D. M., 2007, *Studying History*, Palgrave Study Skills, Basingstoke: Palgrave Macmillan, third edn., pg. 91.

What is the problem with trying to define sources as 'primary' or 'secondary'?

Analysing the sources in the prescribed subjects for question 3

Select the prescribed subject you are studying.

Look at the following documents. Apply the questions set out on page 34 and find the origin and purpose of each source along with one value and one limitation relating to the origin and purpose.

Prescribed subject 1

Source D

Memorandum on Germany and disarmament by Brigadier Temperley, circulated to the British cabinet in 1933.

Within a few weeks of his arrival, Hitler has carried out a revolution and made himself complete master of Germany. The country has given itself up to a delirium of reawakened nationalism and of the most blatant and dangerous militarism. Fuel has been added to the flames by an orgy of military parades and torchlight processions and by a constant stream of patriotic wireless addresses delivered by masters of the art of propaganda, including Hitler himself...

On the military side, Storm detachments of the Nazis and Stahlhelm have been converted into auxiliary police... It has just been announced that the Chancellor has issued a decree calling up all youths... Goering has put a number of air personnel into uniform, and the formation of an air force seems to be actively proceeding... At Geneva the German attitude has stiffened considerably... The increasing insolence of the Germans has brought discussion to a complete standstill... What then is to be our attitude? Are we to go forward as if nothing has happened? Can we afford to ignore what is going on behind the scenes in Germany?

Origin	Value	Limitation
Purpose	Value	Limitation

The origin of this source is valuable in that it was written by a high-ranking military official who would have access to, and may be able to interpret, armaments intelligence that Britain had on Germany.

A limitation of the purpose might be that the Brigadier had an interest in encouraging Britain to pursue rearmament programmes, and the memorandum was to persuade the British cabinet of this in 1933.

Prescribed subject 2

Source E

An extract from Smith, C., 2004, *the Arab-Israeli Conflict*, Boston: Bedford/St Martin's. Smith is a Professor of History at the University of Arizona.

A decisive factor was the news on June 2 that in response to American requests, Nasser had agreed to send his vice president, Zakariya Mohieddine, to Washington on June 7 to discuss measures to defuse the potential for confrontation over the Tiran blockade. This was totally unacceptable, even to Eban, who had resisted the military option until June 1: it was probable that this initiative would aim at a face-saving compromise and that the face to be saved would be Nasser's not Israel's... Egyptian occupation of Sharm al-Sheikh and the blockade might be the reason to justify an attack, but Israel was also determined to deny Nasser his political triumph in the Arab world... With increased confidence in American acquiescence [acceptance], determined to punish Nasser and thwart the intent of Mohieddine's forthcoming visit to Washington, the cabinet on June 4 approved Dayan's plan to attack Egypt the next morning.

Origin	Value	Limitation
Purpose	Value	Limitation

Examiner's hints

A value from the purpose of the source might be that this was intended as an academic analysis for students and a wider audience to better understand the causes and nature of the conflict.

A limitation of the origin of the source is that the book's title seems rather broad in scope and so the book may offer only a broad summary of the key issues involved.

Prescribed subject 3

Source

From the minutes of the meeting of the plenum of the Central Committee of the Communist Party of the Soviet Union, 23 June 1980.

Brezhnev: Not a day goes by when Washington has not tried to revive the spirit of the 'Cold War' to heat up militaristic passions. Any grounds are used for this, real or imagined. One example of this is Afghanistan. The ruling circles of the USA, and of China as well, stop at nothing, including armed aggression, in trying to keep the Afghans from building a new life in accord with the ideals of the revolution of liberation of April 1978. And when we helped our neighbor Afghanistan, at the request of its government, to give a rebuff to aggression, to beat back the attacks of bandit formations which operate primarily from the territory of Pakistan, then Washington and Beijing raised an unprecedented racket. Of what did they accuse the Soviet Union? Of a yearning to break out to warm waters, and an intention to make a grab for foreign oil... In the Soviet act of assistance to Afghanistan there is not a grain of avarice [greed]. We had no choice other than the sending of troops. And the events confirmed that it was the only correct choice.

Origin	Value	Limitation
Purpose	Value	Limitation

Examiner's hints

The origin of the sources is valuable because it is the minutes and therefore exactly what was said at a meeting of an important organ of the Communist government of the Soviet Union. This provides historians with an account of what was said, discussed and decided at this meeting in June 1980 by those in control of events in Afghanistan.

A limitation might be the purpose of the meeting, as it could be to persuade the broader party membership that Brezhnev and the politburo's decision to invade Afghanistan was justified. This might not include an explanation of the real rationale behind the invasion as its purpose was political.

How to approach question 3

Unlike in question 2, you are not asked to compare and contrast the two sources and nor are you asked to make judgments regarding which source is more or less valuable. You only consider the two sources named in the question – you do not talk about any of the other sources on the paper.

Discuss the sources separately. You should end up with four distinct paragraphs covering:

- source A – values
- source A – limitations
- source B – values
- source B – limitations.

Remember the focus of your answer must be on the origin and purpose of each source. Thus, you should concentrate on the information **about** the source rather than the information given **in** the source itself. However, the information in the source may help support your points. For example, if you think that, based on the origin and purpose, the source is likely to be very one-sided, you may find language in the source that supports this point.

Examiner's hints

What *not* to say

Avoid speculating about a source, for example stating: 'the writer might not read German/Arabic/Chinese… and so might have a poor translation of documents'.

Do not focus on possible omissions, for example 'the source doesn't tell us what happened next…' or 'there are ellipses in the source … and therefore we don't know what is missing'.

Nor will you get marks for saying that the source does not have an accurate date, or that we do not know where the historian was born or the city he or she is based in.

Examiner's hint

Where you are given the provenance of a source which is one source embedded in another – for example source A is a **speech by Deng** in 1986, quoted in a secondary school textbook written by Michael Lynch in 1999 – you must evaluate the speech by Deng and not the textbook. You evaluate the speech because that is the **source**. The reference to Lynch is only for copyright purposes and not relevant to your answer.

Activity

Read the following question, source and sample answer. In the answer, the value of the source has been identified thoroughly with full reference to the origins and purpose of the source. Complete the answer by analysing the limitations of the source with reference to its origins and purpose.

Prescribed subject 3

With reference to its origin and purpose, what are the values and limitations of source A for historians studying the fall of the USSR?

Source A

Confidential cable #08144 from the US Embassy, Prague, to the Department of State, 'Demonstrations in Prague and other Czechoslovak cities, November 20,' on 21 November 1989.
From the National Security Archive: www.gwu.edu/~nsarchiv/NSAEBB/NSAEBB141/doc08.pdf

The Prague demonstration of November 20 was the largest yet. The Communist Party daily 'Rude Pravo' admitted to 150,000 people, but embassy officials present thought it closer to 200,000. Police made no attempt to intervene other than to close bridges to prevent the crowd from marching on Prague Castle… Whether as a thorough plan or the result of leadership disagreements, the regime seems to have adopted a carrot and stick strategy, with some conciliatory gestures and a promise of at least economic improvements combined with a none-too-veiled warning of suppression if things remain out of hand. It also is continuing its efforts to taint demonstrators with charges of working for foreign interests. It cannot have been pleased, however, by a Soviet press spokesman statement that described the demonstrations as part of the process of democratization in Eastern Europe… A Czech government spokesman announced that an investigation would be opened on the events of November 17 and whether the police used disproportionate force.

The demonstration appeared to be unorganized and leaderless, and while there has been no call for a gathering today one is generally expected… . Demonstrators voiced anti-communist and anti-government demands, including such slogans as 'Jakes in the wastebasket'.

Sample answer

The origin of the sources is valuable because it is from the US embassy in Prague, so the writer would have access to high-level political sources in Prague during the period leading to the fall of the Communist Party there. Its audience is the US Department of State, so the purpose was to keep the United States informed of developments in Prague. It is an official communication so would be valuable to historians to see what the US interpretation of events was in Prague, and how this was reported back to the US State Department. It might offer an insight into the decisions made by the United States in response. It offers a contemporary opinion of events at the time, by a body that was responsible for gathering information and reporting this back. As it is a confidential report, the information might not be 'censored' to protect a political interest, or limited to avoid diplomatic offence from the communists in Prague or indeed the Soviet Union.

You complete the second part of the evaluation:

_____

_____

_____

_____

_____

_____

_____

_____

_____

Activity

Read through the following statements. These are common in students' answers for this question. Why would they be considered invalid by examiners?

- This source is not useful because the translation could be inaccurate.
- This source is not useful because it doesn't tell us what happened before or after.
- This source is not useful because it is biased.
- This textbook was written over 70 years after the event took place so it is unlikely that the author had first-hand experience. This makes it less useful.
- This is an eyewitness account and so is likely to be reliable.
- This source is only an extract and we don't know what he said next.
- This is a primary source and this makes it very useful.
- As it is an official report, it gives a true representation of what actually happened.

Question 4

This is worth the most marks: 8 of the total 25. It requires you to write a mini-essay. The key to this question is that an **essay** is what is required – not a list of material from each document. However, you are required to **synthesize** material from the documents with your own knowledge into your essay.

How to approach question 4

It is recommended that you plan your answer as you would any essay question. The difference here is that you will use evidence from the documents as well as from your own detailed knowledge to support your arguments.

- First make a brief plan to answer the question based on your own knowledge – you may want to do this in a grid as shown below.
- Then look through the sources and group them into those which support the point in the essay title and those which suggest an alternative argument and add to the grid.
- When you start writing, you will need to write only a brief sentence of introduction.
- When using the sources, refer to the them directly as source A, source E and so on.
- Quote briefly from the sources throughout the essay – a quotation of two or three words is sufficient.
- Use **all** the sources.
- Write a brief conclusion to answer the question.

Example

How far do you agree that that it was 'the intransigence of the French government' (source E) that led to the failure of the disarmament conference?

N.B. This question uses the sources from prescribed subject 1 that you have already seen on page 27 and page 34.

Brief introduction

There were several reasons for the failure of the disarmament conference....

Section 1

Start by analysing the point given in the question title:

Source E puts the blame for the failure of the disarmament conference on France, claiming that France was intransigent.... This is backed up by Izvestia *in source A which claims that 'French imperialism refused to agree to any limitation on armaments'. Also...*

Give any other relevant references to France made in the sources and develop them further with your own knowledge:

France was indeed reluctant to disarm. This was because... (here use your own knowledge to discuss France's fears of Germany which dictated France's actions at the disarmament conference).

When you are in the examination, you could plan this answer out as follows.

Intransigence of the French government	Other factors
Source E... (relevant quotes) Source A...	Source C... Source D... Source B... Source E... N.B. The same source can be used to provide evidence for both sides of the argument.
Own knowledge Reasons for France's fear of Germany were... French actions at conference were...	**Own knowledge** Hitler's aims were... Britain's attitude was...

Activity

Choose your prescribed subject from the list below and sketch out a brief essay plan **from your own knowledge**. For question 4, you will do exactly this – but also, in the examination, you will add in document references to your plan so that you can include material from the sources as evidence for your arguments.

N.B. The references to documents in the plans below are just to show you how to plan the answer and do not refer to documents in this book.

Prescribed subject 1

Using the sources and your own knowledge, analyse how successful the League of Nations was in peacekeeping between 1920 and 1925.

League of Nations successful	League of Nations a failure
Own knowledge: _____ Relevant document/s _____ Own knowledge: _____ Relevant document: _____	Own knowledge: _____ Relevant document/s _____ Own knowledge: _____ Relevant document: _____

Prescribed subject 2

With reference to the sources and your own knowledge, how far do you agree that Britain was responsible for the Suez Crisis in 1956?

Britain responsible	Other countries or factors responsible
Own knowledge: _____ Relevant document/s _____ Own knowledge: _____ Relevant document: _____	Own knowledge: _____ Relevant document/s _____ Own knowledge: _____ Relevant document: _____

Prescribed subject 3

Using the sources and your own knowledge, account for the defeat of the Gang of Four.

Actions of the Gang of Four	Other factors
Own knowledge: _____	Own knowledge: _____
Relevant document/s _____	Relevant document/s _____
Own knowledge: _____	Own knowledge: _____
Relevant document: _____	Relevant document: _____

Examiner's hints

Do not write a list of the contents of each source. Group the sources and synthesize the information of the sources with your own knowledge.

Note that examiners have commented that even in better responses, where a student has used or referred to all five sources, the student does not achieve the highest marks if he or she does not include 'sufficiently detailed own knowledge'.

Again, as with the other questions, responses given as notes in a grid do not reach the higher mark ranges – the grid is for planning purposes only.

If you **only** use the documents or **only** use your own knowledge you can only score a maximum of 5 marks.

Tip

Don't forget to make sure you read the words of the question properly. You need to focus your response to the specific question – this is not an opportunity to write everything you know about the topic. It is a common mistake under pressure to misread the demands of this question. For example, when set the essay question: 'Using the sources and your own knowledge explain why Germany was unhappy with the Treaty of Versailles' many students changed the question to answer: 'To what extent was the Treaty of Versailles a fair and workable Treaty?' This meant that instead of identifying a number of reasons for German discontent with the treaty, the students began to argue that the treaty was fair and that the Germans should **not** have been unhappy with it – but this is not what the question is asking for.

Here is a summary of the key points for each question with the kind of language that is helpful to use in each case.

Question 1 part a

Remember that you have to show your understanding of the source and come up with three points.

Useful sentence starters are:

This source says that….

Secondly…

Thirdly…

It also suggests that…

Question 1 part b

Always start with your key point:

The overall message of this source is that….

This is supported by… (refer here to specific details in the source).

Question 2

This is designed to assess your cross-referencing skills.

When comparing two sources you could use the following structures:

Documents A and B agree that…

Moreover, the two documents are also similar in that… . This is supported by… in source A and… in source B.

For a contrasting paragraph you might write:

Document A differs from document B in that document A says… while document B argues that…

Another difference between the two documents is that…

Moreover, document B goes further than document A when it suggests (or says) that…

Question 3

This question is testing your ability to analyse a source for its value and limitations by looking at its origin and purpose.

Start by talking about the origin and purpose in your opening sentence. This will show the examiner that you are on the right lines and will also get you to think on the right lines.

The origin of this source is… and its purpose is to… , so this document is useful to a historian studying… because (explain how the origin and purpose makes it useful)

or

The origin of this source is valuable because…

The purpose of this source is valuable because…

On the other hand, there are also limitations to using this document for finding out about... This is because (explain how origin and purpose can cause problems for the historian)

or:

The origin of this source makes it less valuable because...

The purpose of this source makes it less valuable because...

Question 4

This is a mini-essay and is assessing your ability to synthesize documents with your own knowledge as well as your ability to present two sides of an argument or to assess the validity of a given statement.

Use the essay writing tips sheet on page 69 for useful vocabulary.

In addition, as you are using documents as well as your own knowledge, you could use the following to help tie in the documents to your own knowledge:

As it says in document C...

This is supported by the information given in documents...

Document A suggests that... and this is supported by the fact that in the Soviet Union at this time...

Historians have argued that... . This viewpoint is supported by the information in document E concerning...

Activity

Read through the May 2010 Paper 1. Choose your prescribed subject.

Make rough notes in answer to each of the four questions and then consider the following.

1 Compare your responses with the sample answers below. What did you do differently? Where were your responses similar? Did you answer each question as thoroughly as this student?
2 What mark would you give the student for each question?
3 How would you improve the student's responses?

Prescribed subject 1

Sample answer

Question 1 part a

According to source A, the significance of Article 16 in the covenant of the League of Nations is that it is used to prevent war between nations of the League and sets up the idea of collective security and economic sanctions as peacekeeping methods. Source A firstly states that 'Should any member of the League resort to war... it shall be deemed to have committed an act of war against all members of the League', which sets up that all nations of the League have to respond to an aggressor as if the aggressor is also at war with them. Secondly, source A states that the League will subject it [the aggressor] to the severance of all trade or financial relations', which thus authorizes complete economic sanctions of the aggressor collectively, which is used to prevent war, and shows the enforcement of both economic sanctions and collective security. Thirdly, it states that in the event of an aggressor state, the League will for 'the prohibition of all exchange between their nationals and the nationals of the covenant-breaking state', and so puts pressure on it to stop its aggressive action. This also shows the idea of collective security as all countries act together.

Examiner's comment

3 marks. Three clear points are made, supported by quotes from the source.

Sample answer

Question 1 part b

The message of source C is that Mussolini, leading Italy, is determined to go to war with Abyssinia, regardless of how the League acts. Mussolini, representing the whole of Italy, is marching down a road with a sign 'to war' with a determined look on his face, and thus he personally wants to go to war. He holds a paper that says 'with the League, without the League, against the League', which is used to convey that regardless of how the League acts, he is going to war, even if that means going 'without the League'.

Examiner's comment

2 marks. The overall message is clear and supported by details from the cartoon.

Sample answer

Question 2

Sources B and D agree that Britain's policy was guided by its fear that Italy and Mussolini would attack it. Source B states that the prime minister of Britain 'explained the great gravity of the European situation, including the danger that Mussolini might make a "mad dog" attack on the British fleet' and source D states 'Hoare and Laval apparently believed that Mussolini might go to war against Britain if Britain should impose an oil sanction.' Sources B and D also agree that other League members did not act as well as they could have, and that the failure of the Abyssinia crisis cannot be laid only on Britain. Source B states that Britain was 'bound to consider where we could rely on effective support from any other member of the League', while source D agrees when it states 'the Assembly refused to take the one decisive measure which would have halted the invasion – the prohibition of the exports of oil to Italy'. Thus the assembly of the League was responsible for the failure of the response instead of just Britain.

However, source B disagrees with source D on a couple of points. Firstly, source B expresses that Britain's policy was also affected by the fact that Britain felt 'bound to consider whether we could rely on effective support from any other members of the League', while source D disagrees as it states that in fact 'the other League members were not backward in imposing sanctions against Italy'. Therefore, source B believes Britain was affected by the weakness of the other members, while source D believes the other members acted well and British policy was not affected by the other members. Source B also states that 'the League's policy is still the policy of the (British) government', and thus claims that British policy is bound to the League of Nations policy to prevent war, while source D disagrees by stating 'it was more important to have Mussolini as an ally against Hitler than to defend Haile Selassie', which means British policy acted more in self-interest than to defend the League. Source B also states that the British would be willing to use harsher measures, but feared a war with Italy would hurt diplomatically the integrity of Europe, and its policy was guided by this fact. It states 'though the results of [an irrational attack on the British fleet] must in the long run be the defeat of Italy, the war might… produce both losses and diplomatic complications of a serious kind', and so Britain's reluctance to get involved was also motivated by its fear that war with Italy would have an impact on the international community. Source D disagrees with this, believing that 'Laval's main foreign policy aim was to maintain an alliance with Italy' instead of upholding the League's rules and protecting the diplomatic ties between nations.

Examiner's comment

6 marks. Good linkage between the sources and a range of similarities and differences are discussed with explicit reference to the sources.

Question 3

Source D is an extract from a book called *Africa in War and Peace* by an author who was in Africa during the crisis and served in the British Army in Africa during the Second World War. The purpose of source D is to analyse Africa during times of war and peace.

The source's origin is valuable in studying the Abyssinian crisis. As the writer was in Africa during the crisis, he understands how Africa and Abyssinia responded to it, and had access to many contemporary opinions and facts about the crisis. Also, as he wrote the book in 2004, he has access to a wide variety of sources published after the crisis, and so can use both a contemporary understanding and revelations later on to give a thorough analysis of the crisis. The purpose of the source, to inform a wider audience about Africa, also makes it valuable. To make it credible it would have been edited and fact checked, or else it would not have been published so it should be historically accurate, making it a valuable source to study.

However, the origin also means that source D has some limitations. As the author was in Africa at the time and served in Africa during the Second World War, it is possible that he mostly sympathizes with Abyssinia rather than with the other countries involved in the crisis, and so his critique of the role of other countries might be marred by this. Also, he was not actually in Abyssinia at the time, but in another part of Africa.

The purpose of source D also gives it some limitations. As the crisis is viewed through the lens of Africa, it is possible that it does not have deep analysis or understanding of the actions of the countries inside Europe, such as Italy, and so could be see as not giving a complete analysis of the crisis. Also, the book's topic is large and unfocused, as it covers on an entire continent and a wide time frame, and is not concentrating on the Abyssinia crisis. This means it will be less useful for finding about this crisis in detail.

The origin of source E is of a speech given by the leader of Abyssinia, Haile Selassie, to the League of Nations towards the end of the crisis. The purpose is to give Selassie's opinion of the League actions during the crisis to the League.

The origin of source E has several values. It firstly is a speech given by the leader of Abyssinia – he is heavily involved in the crisis and has a great knowledge of the events of the crisis. It also is given just before the crisis ends, and so contemporary knowledge and understanding of the event back up Selassie's points. It is also given at the League of Nations, an international organization, and has to be good to convince the other members of Selassie's opinion.

The purpose of source D also makes it valuable. Selassie is representing his nation, which is under attack by Italy, and he has to be convincing and have good knowledge in order to get support for his country.

However, the origin of the speech also has limitations. As it is given by the leader of one of the countries directly involved in the crisis, it of course is going to be heavily slanted in favour of that country rather than giving an objective overview and opinion of the event.

The purpose also has its limitations. As there is a motive to the speech, to convince the audience that Haile Selassie's view are right, he uses only comments that support his viewpoint so that he sounds more convincing, giving a less objective view of the event.

Examiner's comment

6 marks. Value and limitation of both sources are considered with good reference to the origin and purpose of the sources.

Question 4

The League failed to act enough to prevent Italy from taking Abyssinia, in part due to the difficulty of applying its policy of collective security. This could be seen as due to the context of British foreign policy, of Italy's determination, or the fact that the League did not have a strong enough mandate to utilize collective security.

Source B states that British foreign policy meant that Britain, a major player of the League, could not act enough and so it was difficult to utilize collective security. Source B states that 'the great gravity of the European situation, including the danger that Mussolini might make a "mad dog" attack on the British fleet', meant Britain was hesitant to act, and so collective security could not be utilized effectively.

Source D also agrees that the complications of British foreign policy meant it could not act to support collective security. More specifically, it states: 'In 1935 Laval's main foreign policy aim was to maintain an alliance with Italy, so it was more important to have Mussolini as an ally against Hitler than to defend Haile Selassie.' Thus British self-interest in foreign policy meant it could not jeopardize its relationship with Italy to act in the context of collective security. Mussolini was an ideal ally against Hitler, who had walked out of the Geneva disarmament conference in 1933 and in 1934 stated that he was going to rearm Germany. Mussolini had blocked Hitler's attempt at Anschluss in 1934, and through this had shown himself to be a good ally to Britain against Hitler. As Britain feared Nazi Germany under Hitler, who had also left the League in 1933, it was more likely to act to preserve ties with Italy (with which Britain formed the Stresa front against Hitler in 1935) than to act in collective security. As key members

acted in self-interest rather than in collective security, nations could not rely on each other to isolate an aggressor and so it was impossible for collective security to truly work.

However, it could also be seen that Italy did not care how the League acted, and so collective security was not viable in the first place. Source C believes that Mussolini would have gone to war 'without the League', and so did not care about how it acted. The Great Depression that had started in 1929 had economically weakened fascist Italy, and Mussolini, whose Italy had suffered, had to go to war to get a foreign policy victory regardless of the League.

Another important point is that the weakness of the League's collective security also made it hard to take effective action. Source A states that the League calls upon 'effective military, naval or air force' from 'members of the League'. However, as no country would really willingly give up its military to an international organization, the idea of collective security could not work.

In conclusion, British foreign policy was the biggest reason, as it was a major player of the League, and its reluctance to act doomed the idea of collective security.

Examiner's comment

7 marks. All sources used effectively, apart from source E, which is not mentioned. Own knowledge is also incorporated though it could be extended more in some places. The answer is structured well and answers the question.

Prescribed subject 2

Sample answer

Question 1 part a
It appears from source A that the UN Partition Plan of 1947 wanted Jerusalem to be in an internationally administered zone 'corpus seperatum'. There would be an Arab state and a Jewish state, each independent of each other.

Examiner's comment
2 marks. There are two valid points, but the student has not offered three clear points here.

Sample answer

Question 1 part b
The reactions to the plan were divided. The pro-Jewish state Zionists were pleased with the plan, but the Arab peoples were not happy with it at all. Both sides committed barbaric acts during this time.

Examiner's comment
1 mark; for 2 marks the second point needs detailed development.

Sample answer

Question 2

Both sources talk of violence against civilians in Deir Yassin; source C 'they shot whoever they saw' and source D 'civilians suffered inevitable casualties'. Source D supports the view in source C that there were deaths on both the Jewish side and the Arab side. However, source C gives numbers of deaths of both the Irgun and the Arabs, but source D does not. Finally, source D goes into the aftermath and results of the battle, but source C only says what happened during it.

Examiner's comment
4 marks. Some valid comparisons and contrasts are made. The student needs to develop details, and more contrasts should be identified.

Sample answer

Question 3

The origin of source C is that it is written by a member of the Haganah who was there at Deir Yassir. The purpose of this document was probably to inform officially what he had seen happen. It is valuable as it is an eyewitness account and can give us an insight into what happened from his point of view. He was an important person on the Israeli side, therefore his opinion counts. The limitations of the source is that this was probably emotional for him, and his view was probably one-sided. He might have forgotten important information as the source was written a year after the violence occurred.

The value of source E is that it is a well-written book by a history teacher, it is recently written and it has hindsight. Its purpose is to reflect on events and analyse them. A limitation is that the writer was not there at the time.

Examiner's comment
3 marks. Some valid evaluation of the first source. Lacks valid comment on the second, particularly on limitations. The student does not include an evaluation of the purpose of each document.

Sample answer

Question 4

The reason for the 'flight of the Palestinian Arabs during the civil war between 1947 and 1948' was fear of the Israelis. The documents show that there was much violence against the Arabs during this time and this was a key factor in their flight.

From source A it could be seen that they left because there was pressure from the UN to give too much land and benefits to the Jews. But, more importantly, the fighting and death of civilians caused terror among the Palestinians, as seen in documents B and C: 'they shot whoever they saw'. This reason can also be found in document D as its says that the bloodshed in the village was so terrifying to the Arabs that it was 'worth a dozen battalions' to the Israelis. Finally, document E adds a different reason for their flight: it argues that it might have been due to the Arab leaders encouraging them to go.

In conclusion, although they were unhappy with the UN plan, and their leaders were encouraging them to flee, it was the violence that was the key factor in the civil war that made the Palestinians leave.

Examiner's comment
4 marks. Uses all the documents to analyse the question – but should have more detailed development. Lacks detailed own knowledge.

Prescribed subject 3

N.B. The sample answer to question 1 part a is missing as the IB will not reprint the source for this question due to copyright issues.

Sample answer

Question 1 part b

The overall message of this cartoon is that Deng has destroyed any hope of democracy in China. This can be seen by the fact that the statue of liberty has been beheaded by Deng. His axe is very large and signifies the size of the force that has been used to stop democracy.

Examiner's comment

2 marks. The overall message is clear with good development using the details of the cartoon.

Sample answer

Question 2

Sources A and C are similar because they both say that Deng wanted to carry out 'modernisations'. In source A, Deng talks about a huge 'effort' to try and 'accomplish the Four Modernisations. This willingness to change is also illustrated in source C which states that Deng wanted to 'create a new era'. Another similarity between the sources is that they both say that Deng wanted intellectuals to discuss new ideas to bring the revolution forward. Source A talks about 'path breakers who dare to think' and source C says that Mao rehabilitated 'hundreds of thousands of intellectuals' and declared a 'new era of openness'.

However, there are also differences between the sources. In source A Deng states that he wants 'democracy'. However, in source C we learn that Deng arrested people for writing on the democracy wall, thereby showing 'the limits of his toleration'. Another difference is that source C states that there was an 'outpouring of Chinese emotion and criticism of the Communist system' but this is not mentioned at all by Deng in source A.

Examiner's comment

6 marks. There is a clear link between the sources and succinct quotes to support points.

Sample answer

Question 3

The origin and purpose of source A make this source valuable for several reasons. Firstly, the origin of the source is Deng himself so it gives us an insight into his aims on modernisation. He is giving a speech and the purpose is to inspire the workers with his vision of what the Four Modernisations can achieve so this tells us what he wants the workers to believe regarding his aims. However, this also makes it limited in its purpose. He would want to convince his audience of the need to make the Four Modernisations work and so he could be exaggerating or even lying (for instance over his promises of democracy) in order to inspire his audience. It could just be propaganda to reinforce the fact that the Chinese Communist Party is democratic.

The origin and purpose of source C makes it very valuable to a historian studying Deng's aims.

This is because it comes from a historian who is lecturer in history and whose purpose would thus be to give a detailed and presumably objective account of the history of China. He would therefore be committed to carrying out thorough research. As he is based in the UK, he would not be subjected to any censorship and as the book was published in 2003, enough time has elapsed since 1978 to allow a full evaluation of Deng's aims and to have various documents available. However, there are also limitations to this source. The title of the book means that its purpose is to cover the whole of Chinese history and so there would probably only be a limited section on Deng's aims. Also, it is possible that the historian would not have had full access to all the documents on this period as China is still communist and has not given historians full access to the archives.

Examiner's comment

6 marks. Valid points are made on both value and limitations with reference to the origin and purpose.

Sample answer

Question 4

In carrying out the Four Modernisations, Deng was successful in achieving the modernisation of China; however, he failed to achieve his aims regarding the democracy of China and indeed ended up being very repressive, as illustrated with the massacre of Tiananmen Square.

With regard to the modernisations of agriculture and industry, Deng was very successful in ridding China of its 'backwardness' (source A) by encouraging more foreign trade to improve China's industry. In addition to this, Deng implemented his 'hands-off' policy in the economy, which liberalized Chinese industry more and allowed farmers in agriculture to move away from the communes. By allowing foreign trade and giving Chinese farmers and business owners more freedom, Deng was able to play a key role in 'transforming the Chinese economy' (source D).

Deng also made progress in the 'science and technology modernisation' by fostering ties with the United States (source C).

However, Deng was not so successful with democracy. Despite his promises of 'a full measure of democracy', Deng did not allow any freedoms and clamped down on those who wrote on the democracy wall. This repression led to the Tiananmen Square movement ending in a massacre and the end of all hopes of democracy, as indicated by source B. As source E indicates, Deng was successful in stopping any move to democracy rather than encouraging it.

Examiner's comment

6 marks. The sources have been used well to form the basis of the points made. However, own knowledge is a bit thin; for example, there could be development of the economic reforms carried out by Deng.

Practice Paper 1 questions

Now you can test out the skills you have been learning and practising in this chapter. Choose one of the following examples of a Paper 1 to answer in full. You should attempt to do this under real examination conditions.

You have 5 minutes of reading time. (Do not write during this time.)

You have one hour to complete all four questions.

Prescribed subject 1

The following sources relate to the refusal of the United States to join the League of Nations.

Source A

Speech by Henry Cabot Lodge to the US Senate, 12 August 1919.

What is the result of all this? We are in the midst of all the affairs of Europe. We have joined in alliance with all European concerns. We have joined in alliance with all the European nations which have thus far joined the league, and all nations which may be admitted to the league. We are sitting there dabbling in their affairs and intermeddling in their concerns. In other words, Mr President – and this comes to the question which is fundamental with me – we have forfeited and surrendered, once and for all, the great policy of 'no entangling alliances' upon which the strength of this Republic has been founded for 150 years...

There is another and even more commanding reason why I shall record my vote against this treaty. It imperils what I conceive to be the underlying, the very first principles of this Republic. It is in conflict with the right of our people to govern themselves free from all restraint, legal or moral, foreign powers… I will not, I cannot, give up my belief that America must… be permitted to live her own life… All plans, however ambitious and fascinating they seem in their proposal, but which embarrass or entangle and impede her sovereign will, which would prevent her freedom of action, I unhesitatingly put behind me…

Source B

A cartoon from the British magazine, Punch, 10 December 1919.

THE GAP IN THE BRIDGE.

Source C

Lefaber, W., Polenberg, R. and Woloch, N., 1992, *The American Century: A history of the United States since 1941*, New York: McGraw Hill, fourth edn.

When President Wilson returned to the USA, he found three groups preparing to fight against him. One, led by Senator Lodge, was determined to defeat anything Wilson recommended. A second group was made up of progressives like Herbert Hoover. This group did not personally dislike Wilson (Hoover had been one of Wilson's advisers in Paris), but it was afraid that the League of Nations' covenant would reduce the control Congress had over domestic affairs. A third group, led by Republican William Botah of Idaho, refused to agree to American participation in any international organisation. One common thread united the three groups. All wanted to maintain maximum American freedom of action in the world, particularly so that Americans could freely take advantage of their new economic power without having to worry about political restraints.

Source D

Woodrow Wilson defending the Treaty of Versailles in a speech, 1919.

I want to remind you how the permanency of peace is at the heart of this treaty. This is not merely a treaty of peace with Germany… it is nothing less than world settlement, and at the centre of that stands the covenant for the future we call the Covenant of the League of Nations. Without it the treaty can not be worked and without it is a mere temporary arrangement with Germany. The Covenant of the League of Nations is the instrumentality [means] for the maintenance of peace.

If the treaty is not ratified by the Senate, the war will have been fought in vain, and the world will be thrown into chaos. I promised our soldiers, when I asked them to take up arms, that it was a war to end wars…

Source E

Traynor, J., 1991, *Europe 1890–1990*, Nashville TN: Thomas Nelson.

The power of the League of Nations to resolve [the disputes of the 1920s] was not always apparent. In the absence of the US – whose Senate finally rejected the Versailles Treaty in March 1920 – it was essential that the remaining powers were in agreement of major issues. This was by no means the case. Indeed, Ruth Henig points out that the 'repudiation by the United States of the entire peace settlement increased the reluctance of successive British governments in the 1920s to underwrite in any tangible way the European territorial settlement'. In the dispute between Turkey and Greece of 1920–23, Britain and France took opposite sides. While France endorsed Poland's aims in Russia and Silesia, Britain pointedly did not. In addition, the distractions caused by major problems in Ireland and the Empire made it impossible for Britain to concentrate on upholding the interest of the League before national concerns. While France fretted about Germany, Britain sought to redevelop trade links with her former enemy.

1 a What reasons are given in source A as to why the United States should not join the League of Nations?
[3 marks]

1 b What is the message of source B?
[2 marks]

2 Compare and contrast the reasons given in sources A and C concerning the reasons for the United States not joining the League of Nations.
[6 marks]

3 With reference to origin and purpose, discuss the value and limitations of sources B and D for historians studying the impact of American attitudes towards the League of Nations.
[6 marks]

4 Using the sources and your own knowledge, analyse the results of the United States' absence in the League of Nations on international events in the 1920s.
[8 marks]

Prescribed subject 2

These sources relate to the Suez crisis of 1956.

Source A

Extract of a speech made by President Nasser, 28 July 1956.

The uproar which we anticipated has been taking place in London and Paris. This tremendous uproar is not supported by reason or logic. It is backed only by imperialist methods, by the habits of blood-sucking and of usurping rights, and by interference in the affairs of other countries. An unjustified uproar arose in London, and yesterday Britain submitted a protest to Egypt. I wonder what was the basis of this protest by Britain to Egypt? The Suez Canal Company is an Egyptian company, subject to Egyptian sovereignty. When we nationalized the Suez Canal Company, we only nationalized an Egyptian limited company, and by doing so we exercised a right which stems from the very core of Egyptian sovereignty. What right has Britain to interfere in our internal affairs?

Source B

A cartoon by David Low, published in the Manchester *Guardian*, 6 November 1956.

"ME, TOO!"

Source C

Extract from the Sèvres Protocol, October 1956, taken from Turner, B., 2006, *Suez: The first oil war*, London: Hodder and Stoughton, pg. 297.

1 The Israeli forces launch in the evening of 29 October 1956 a large scale attack on the Egyptian forces with the aim of reaching the canal zone the following day.

2 On being apprised [informed] of these events, the British and French governments during the day of 30 October 1956 respectively and simultaneously make two appeals to the Egyptian and the Israeli government on the following lines:

  A. TO THE EGYPTIAN GOVERNMENT
  a) halt all acts of war
  b) withdraw all its troops ten miles from the Canal
  c) accept temporary occupation of key positions on the Canal by the Anglo-French forces to guarantee freedom of passage to the vessels of all nations until a final settlement.

  B. TO THE ISRAELI GOVERNMENT
  a) halt all acts of war
  b) withdraw all its troops ten miles to the east of the Canal.

  C. The representatives of the three governments agree that the Israeli Government will not be required to meet the conditions in the appeal addressed to it, in the event that the Egyptian Government does not accept those in the appeal addressed to it for their part.

3 In the event that the Egyptian Government should fail to agree within the stipulated time to the conditions... the Anglo-French forces will launch military operations against the Egyptian forces in the early hours of the morning of 31 October.

Source D

Eden, A., 1906, *Full Circle*, London: Cassell.

On October 25th the Cabinet discussed the specific possibility of conflict between Israel and Egypt and decided in principle how it would react if this occurred. The Governments of France and the United Kingdom should, it considered, at once call on both parties to stop hostilities and withdraw their forces to a distance from either bank of the canal. If one or both failed to comply within a definite period, then the British and French forces would intervene as a temporary measure to separate the combatants... Our purpose was to safeguard free passage through the canal, if it were threatened with becoming a zone of warfare, and to arrest the spread of fighting in the Middle East.'

Source E

Turner, B., 2006, *Suez: The first oil war*, London: Hodder and Stoughton, pg. 299.

According to Dayan, the Israeli and Anglo-French objectives were different but parallel. The Anglo-French goal was to hold the Suez Canal to ensure free passage while Israel intended to take control of the western shore of the Gulf of Aqaba and Sharm el-Sheikh to secure freedom of shipping. The first objective was a temporary measure, the second permanent. The first was to be achieved with Israeli support, the second by Israel alone... At 10:30 pm on 24 October...[a] copy of the Sevres Protocol was handed over to Eden, who showed surprise and then anger that secret diplomacy was no longer a matter of a handshake between gentlemen. It was the defining moment of the Suez crisis. Whatever justification was later advanced for Eden's policy on Suez, it foundered on this simple fact – that the prime minister was thrown into a panic by the risk of his actions becoming known outside a closed circle of senior colleagues who could be trusted...'

1 **a** Identify the key reasons for British involvement in Suez made by Eden in source D. [3 marks]

1 **b** What is the cartoonist's message in source B regarding foreign intervention in Egypt? [2 marks]

2 Compare and contrast the views expressed in source A and source E on British involvement in the Suez crisis. [6 marks]

3 With reference to origin and purpose, discuss the value and limitations of sources C and E for a historian studying the reasons for the Suez crisis of 1956. [6 marks]

4 Using the sources and your own knowledge, explain the events that led to the Suez crisis of 1956. [8 marks]

Prescribed subject 3

These sources relate to impact of Deng's reforms on China 1978–1989.

Source A

Lynch, M., 2008, *The People's Republic of China 1949–76*, London: Hodder and Stoughton, pg. 167.

For many Chinese people, the reforms introduced by the Deng in the period 1979–1989 proved deeply disappointing… Students and intellectuals felt that, despite the promise of progress and reform held out by the modernisation programme, the Communist Party under Deng Xioping had failed to deliver.

Poor job prospects were a particular anxiety among the students. In the late 1970s, in accordance with the Four Modernisations programme, there had been an explosion in the numbers entering higher education. But a decade later it was evident that employment opportunities had failed to keep pace with the rising number of graduates. There was resentment that such jobs as were available were reserved for party members and their children. It was this grievance that fuelled the anger over government corruption.

Source B

Cartoon by Nicholas Garland, published in the *Independent* newspaper, 16 June 1989.
The figure in front of the tank is Deng.

www.cartoons.ac.uk/record/NG3961

Source C

Zhang Gong (political commissar and Director of the Political Department of a certain martial law unit) giving a statement at a press conference called by the Chinese Communist Party officials two days after the government crackdown. Excerpt from Yuan Mu's television news conference, 6 June 1989. Translation copyright 1990, ME Sharpe Inc.

First, I wish to explain a question to our comrades in the journalistic circles in a responsible manner. Through you, I also wish to see to it that the people in the capital and all other parts of the country can clearly understand the question I am going to explain. Between 4.00 am and 8.30 pm on June 3rd… the [martial law] units absolutely did not kill one single student or individual. No one was killed at that time. Nor was there a single person killed or injured because he was run over by our vehicle.

(Zhang then talks about the operation to clean up Tiananmen Square.)

We again broadcast the urgent announcement, so that more people could leave the square before the troops formally cleaned up the square. As a result of our repeated broadcasts, some representatives of the student organizations asked our martial law units whether the students could peacefully or voluntarily withdraw from the square. The marital law units promptly accepted their request and, through loud speakers, again explained to the students that their request had been accepted. In our broadcasts, we kept asking the students to leave the square voluntarily and peacefully. Thus, quite a number of students began to leave the square from the southeast exit.

Source D

A report on Tiananmen Square written by Louise Doder, a Western reporter in Beijing, on 12 June 1989, taken from Doder, L., 1989, 'A bloodbath in Beijing', *Maclean's*, June 1989.

The troops forced their way into Tiananmen behind armoured personnel carriers and tanks. They first fired off tracer bullets and tear gas, while loudspeaker messages warned the tens of thousands of students to leave. Then they opened fire directly on the crowd and charged them with bayonets, killing – according to initial reports – hundred of demonstrators, leaving others wounded and causing mass panic… The huge crowd desperately sought safety in the side streets leading from Tiananmen, shouting 'Bandits, bandits!'. Even there, the troops continued to fire on them, as screams of terror filled the area.

Source E

Hsu, I., 2008, *The Rise of Modern China 1949–76*, New York: Oxford University Press, fourth edn., pg. 167.

Deng Xiaoping was a curious mixture of economic progressivism and political conservatism endowed with a gift for playing a balancing act as political necessity dictated. In a system where the rule of man superseded the rule of law, he was the supreme arbiter. In his mind, economic reforms and an open-door policy were but means by which to borrow foreign technology, capital and managerial skills. These were seen as tools with which to strengthen Communist rule, but never as steps to move the country toward a Western-style democracy… . The country could not tolerate any disruption, such as student turmoil, or any disturbing influence, such as Western liberalism. In short he was interested in Western science, but not Western values.

1 a What reasons does source A suggest for student discontent in the 1980s?

[3 marks]

1 b What is the message of source B?

[2 marks]

2 Compare and contrast sources C and D regarding the account of what actions were taken by the army in Tiananmen Square on 3 June 1989. [6 marks]

3 With reference to their origin and purpose, assess the value and limitations of sources B and C for historians studying the Tiananmen Square massacre. [6 marks]

4 Using the sources and your own knowledge, analyse the extent to which Deng reformed China between 1978 and 1989. [8 marks]

Essay writing

'Most historians say that the research is the fun bit and that writing is a struggle.'

JEREMY BLACK AND DONALD MACRAILD, *STUDYING HISTORY*

Papers 2 and 3 of your IB Diploma Programme history examination are assessed through essay writing, so a large part of your history course will be devoted to practising essay writing, both in non-timed and in timed conditions.

Why is so much weight put on this particular form of assessment? Because the essay is key for demonstrating your historical knowledge and understanding, along with your ability to analyse and to form a judgment.

As you will see from the marking criteria for Papers 2 and 3, IB essays assess all of the IB history assessment objectives:

- Objective 1: **Knowledge and understanding**
- Objective 2: **Application and interpretation**
- Objective 3: **Synthesis and evaluation**
- Objective 4: **Use of historical skills.** For essays this means your ability to structure an essay effectively so that it addresses the question using the skills above.

(Refer back to page 5 for an outline of what each of the objectives involves.)

To attain these assessment objectives, a good essay will:

- indicate a firm historical knowledge and evidence of wide reading
- include a relevant selection of information
- analyse the key points
- reach a judgment on the question set
- be clearly structured.

Steps to writing a good essay

'History essays are an art form, but they also benefit from an underpinning of scientific method; that is, they benefit from your development of a logical and reasoned approach to writing, construction and organisation.'

JEREMY BLACK AND DONALD MACRAILD, *STUDYING HISTORY*

There are several key steps in writing an essay.

Understanding the question

Your first task in writing an essay is to understand what the question is asking. You have to 'deconstruct' the question. This means focusing on each part of the question, as follows.

- The **topic** – what overall issue or topic is the question focused on?
- Any **dates** that are given – how will this affect your answer?
- Key **concepts or specific factors** – these may need defining to make sense of your answer.
- The **'command' words** giving the instructions of what you have to do. Sometimes you may have two sets of instructions in one question (see below).

Each part is vital to understanding what the question is asking. If you misunderstand any of the components, you may start off on the wrong track.

For example, the following questions can be broken down as follows.

How successful were Stalin's domestic policies in the period 1928–1941?

Topic	Stalin
Dates	1928–1941
Key concepts or specific factors	domestic policies
Command words	How successful?

How far can the Gulf War, 1990–1991, be considered an example of a limited war?

Topic	Gulf War
Dates	1990–1991
Key concepts or specific factors	limited war
Command words	How far can… be considered an example?

For Paper 2, you may have the extra challenge of having to choose your own examples (and therefore your own dates). In addition, your case studies may have to be taken from different regions (see the example below).

Analyse the importance of air power in two wars, each chosen from a different region.

Topic	air power in war
Examples	wars from two different regions
Key concepts or specific factors	air power
Command words	Analyse the importance of…

In pairs, break down the following questions in the same way as the examples given. You could use different colours to highlight the key parts of each question.

Paper 2 questions

1   Assess the significance of Gandhi's leadership and methods in the struggle for Indian independence.

2   In what ways and with what results was Berlin the focus of Cold War problems between 1948-1961?

3   Select two leaders of single party states, each chosen from a different region, and explain how and why economic factors helped them to rise to power.

4   Assess the extent to which the main political and economic developments in Japan (1945–1952) were the result of Cold War fears. (Topic 2, November 2010) © IB Organization 2010

Paper 3 questions

1   Assess the successes and failures of Mussolini's economic, religious and social policies between 1922 and 1939.

2   Compare and contrast the ways in which imperial China and Japan responded to the challenges posed by the arrival of Western powers in the early- to mid-nineteenth century. (November 2010)

© IB Organization 2010

3   Analyse the factors that contributed to the economic success of Japan in the second half of the twentieth century. (November 2010) © IB Organization 2010

4   To what extent was the outbreak of revolution in France in 1789 caused by the actions of Louis XVI?

5   Analyse the major causes of instability in Palestine between 1917 and 1939. (November 2010)

© IB Organization 2010

6   Evaluate the reasons for the formation of NATO and the impact of its policies up to 2000. (May 2010) © IB Organization 2010

7   Contrast the roles and policies of Dr Martin Luther King and Malcolm X in the development of the Civil Rights Movement in the United States. (November 2010) © IB Organization 2010

8   In what ways did apartheid, as developed between 1948 and 1960, differ from earlier racial policies in South Africa? (November 2010) © IB Organization 2010

9   Compare and contrast the impact of British colonial rule on Kenya and Tanganyika. (November 2010) © IB Organization 2010

Command words

The next step is to understand the meaning of the command words. Below is a list of common command words and an explanation of what you are expected to do in answering the question.

Explanation questions	
Command word/s	You are expected to:
Why...?	give the causes of an event
Explain/Account for...	give reasons for the causes or results of an event
Evaluative or assessment questions	
Command word/s	You are expected to:
To what extent (How far)...? How far do you accept the view that...?	examine the merits of a particular view or argument and weigh this against an alternative view or argument, finally reaching a conclusion
Analyse...	examine in detail the different elements or factors
Assess the influence of...	make a judgment as to the influence of an event or person

How successful… ?	make a judgment as to how successful an event or person was
Discuss	examine in detail an issue or argument presenting a range of arguments and evidence
Compare and contrast…	examine the similarities and differences between two or more people or events
Consider the validity of…	examine the argument and decide whether it can be justified based on the evidence
Evaluate…	reach a judgment by examining strengths and limitations

Activity

In pairs, look back at the questions that you analysed on page 60. Using your breakdown of the key parts, and the explanation above of the command words, explain orally to your partner exactly what you have to do to answer each of the questions.

Find essay titles from the topics that you are studying on Paper 2 and repeat the same exercise.

Key concepts or words

Sometimes the questions will contain key concepts or key words that will need defining if your answer is to make sense. In the question on page 59 about the Gulf War 1990–1991, for example, you need to give a definition of 'limited war', so that you can then discuss whether the Gulf War fits the definition that you have given.

Activity

Below is a list of common concepts and words that can come up in essay questions. Write a clear definition for each one.

total war	right wing	economic
limited war	opportunist	social
guerrilla war	tyrant	ideology
fascist	radical	authoritarian
communist	idealist	
left wing	political	

Dealing with quotations

When you are given a quotation to comment on, you need to break it down in the same way as you break down a question – topic, dates, examples, key concepts or specific factors, command words.

Example

'The overthrow of Communist regimes in Central and Eastern Europe would not have succeeded without strong, charismatic leaders.' With reference to two leaders, to what extent do you agree with this statement?

(Topic 4, November 2010) © IB Organization

Topic	Overthrow of Communist regimes
Dates	1989–1990
Examples	two leaders
Key concepts or specific factors	strong, charismatic leaders
Command words	to what extent…?

Examiner's hint

Note that some questions will have more than one set of commands, for example:

Analyse the nature of the Cold War and **explain why**, in spite of serious crises, it did not turn into a third world war. (November 2003)

© IB Organization

In what ways and **for what reasons** did technological developments affect the nature and the outcome of two twentieth-century wars, each chosen from a different region? (November 2010)

© IB Organization

(Notice that this not only has two sets of commands but also two factors to deal with.)

Planning

Once you have an understanding of the essay question, you can start to plan your essay.

Why is a plan so important?

- You need to have a clear argument (see page 65) sorted out in your head before you start writing the essay. You will need to set this argument out in your introduction and state it again in your conclusion.
- A plan will allow you to see if your argument works – to see if you have enough evidence to support it.
- It will allow you to sort out your key paragraphs and decide in which order to present them.
- It will make writing your essay faster.
- It will help cut out waffle and repetition.
- If you get in the habit of writing a plan, you will find it easier to do this in the examination, which will in turn help you to organize your thinking and your time under pressure.

The detail included in a plan will change according to whether you are writing the essay for a class assignment, as a revision exercise, or as a timed essay in examination conditions.

Below is an example of the kind of plan that you might set out for a class assignment.

To what extent was Nicholas II responsible for the February revolution of 1917?

Introduction incorporating key argument

Nicholas was important – character, actions before the First World War started, actions during the war. But the First World War was key for bringing Russia to the revolutionary situation and for highlighting the inadequacies of Nicholas II.

Paragraph 1

Nicholas's actions prior to the First World War had already alienated key elements of society:
- his failure to keep the promise of the October manifesto; Fundamental Law, Stolypin's reign of terror, Electoral Law of 1907
- '... the support base of the autocratic regime was very narrow in 1914' Martin McCauley.

Paragraph 2

At the outbreak of war, Nicholas II further alienated the middle classes and the Duma:
- refusing to cooperate with Zemstvos and the Union of Municipal Councils (Zengor)
- rejecting Duma's proposal for 'ministry of national confidence'.

Paragraph 3

Nicholas made several key mistakes during the course of the war which further alienated the Russian people:
- taking over command of the army – impact
- putting Rasputin in charge – impact.

Paragraph 4

However, the impact of the war was key for creating a revolutionary situation in Russia:

- military disasters and losses
- inflation
- fuel and bread shortages in cities
- Norman Stone – the First World War was key – Russia might have survived if it hadn't been for the war
- Michael Florinsky – without war, Russia could have continued to progress 'along the road that had been followed by other countries'.

Examiner's hints

When planning, make sure you keep your notes and history textbook close at hand to be able to check easily for evidence.

Include any relevant quotes from historians in your plan.

The introduction

The introduction is a key part of your essay. In your introduction you will:

- show that you understand the question; this could involve referring to the dates set or events mentioned in the title and putting them into context and also explaining any concepts (see page 61)
- indicate the scope of your essay
- set out your line of argument
- provide a transition to the first paragraph of your essay.

The reader (your teacher or examiner) should feel after reading your introduction that you have a good grasp of the key issues connected to the question and a clear line of argument.

Activity

Task 1

Read the following introduction.

Highlight where the student has:

- shown that he or she has understood the question
- set out his or her argument
- allowed for a transition to the next paragraph.

> How far can it be argued that Brezhnev's foreign policy was based on aggression?
>
> During the time that Brezhnev was president of the USSR between 1964 and 1982, the USSR and the USA carried out a policy of 'détente'. This relaxation of tension between the superpowers led to several key agreements in military, economic and political relations. However, despite this easing of hostilities and period of co-operation, it can still be argued that Brezhnev's actions in Africa, Eastern Europe and Afghanistan meant that his foreign policy was based on 'aggression'.

Task 2

Below are three introductions written by students to answer the question: To what extent was the Tet Offensive a turning point in the Vietnam War?

In pairs, discuss what you consider to be the positive and negative points of each introduction. How would you improve on each of the introductions?

Introduction A

The Tet Offensive involved tens of thousands of North Vietnamese troops and Viet Cong attacking cities in South Vietnam on the Tet holiday in 1968. Although it failed in its military aim of causing the Saigon government to collapse, the Tet Offensive did bring about a crisis in the US government. As a result of this offensive, political and public opinion swung against the US involvement in Vietnam. The increase in the number of US troops ended, there was no more talk of 'light at the end of the tunnel', Johnson refused to accept a second nomination to run as President and Nixon was elected with a mandate to bring 'peace with honour'. Thus the Tet Offensive can indeed be seen as a turning point in the war.

Introduction B

In 1968, the VC and NVA launched a major offensive against the cities in Southern Vietnam. This broke the traditional Tet holiday truce and Americans were shocked to see the US Embassy in Saigon being attacked. The offensive caused the death of nearly 4,000 Americans and tens of thousands of Vietnamese. It also caused massive damage to cities such as Hue. This essay will discuss the impact of this battle on American strategy in Vietnam.

Introduction C

US troops arrived in Vietnam in 1965. They then had to fight a guerrilla war against the Viet Cong which was very difficult for the US soldiers as they were not used to fighting against an enemy which was hard to identify and hard to attack in the jungles of Vietnam. In 1967, however, Johnson claimed that there was 'light at the end of the tunnel'. Soon after this, the Vietnamese launched an offensive known as the Tet Offensive and this would lead to a turning point in US policy towards Vietnam.

The main body of your essay: paragraphs

Your essay will probably contain around six paragraphs. Each paragraph should include:

- a clear opening sentence which links to the question and states the key point or argument of the paragraph
- evidence which supports the point given in the first sentence
- a final sentence which sums up the argument of the paragraph and leads on to the next paragraph.

Activity

Opening sentences

Opening sentences are sometimes known as 'signpost' or 'topic' sentences. They are key for establishing the point of the paragraph and leading you into an analytical approach. Examine the sentences below. Which ones would act as 'signpost' sentences?

To what extent was Hitler responsible for the Second World War?

- In 1933 Hitler became Chancellor of Germany.
- The Hossbach memorandum provides further evidence that Hitler was planning for war.
- Hitler wrote *Mein Kampf* while he was in prison.
- Hitler invaded Poland in 1939 and then Britain declared war on Germany.
- Hitler's actions in the late 1930s give a clear indication that he was planning for war.
- However, it could be argued that Britain and France played a role in causing the Second World War.

Using evidence

Your opening sentence should set out the argument for your paragraph. You then need to develop this idea further and support it with evidence. Selecting the appropriate evidence is key. Only include information that supports your claim – and make it clear why that piece of information supports your claim – don't leave it for the reader to work out. You need to include 'analytical links' to show how your evidence links to the question.

Statement

Evidence

...this is a history examination and not an invitation to unleash a torrent of generalities'
Subject report, May 2010

Activity

Look at the following example of a paragraph from an answer written to the essay question: **Assess Louis XVI's role in causing the French Revolution.**

> Louis XVI played a key role in causing the French Revolution through his role in bankrupting the government. Louis's agreement to help the Americans in their fight against the British in the American War of Independence cost France approximately 1066 million livres. This money was raised mainly through Necker securing loans which in turn meant that the royal debt increased substantially and with it the amount that had to be paid on interest of the debts each year. By 1786, the government's debts were far greater than its income and this situation created a crisis in the government that was to lead to the calling of the Estates General.

Identify in the paragraph:

- a clear opening sentence which states the key point of the paragraph
- facts supporting the opening sentence (that is, facts showing how Louis XVI helped to bankrupt the government)
- precise but detailed factual evidence including relevant names, statistics and dates
- analytical links, for example 'which in turn meant...', 'this situation created...' and 'that was to lead to...'
- a final sentence which links back to the opening sentence and leads on to the next paragraph.

Sequence of paragraphs

Your sequence of paragraphs should lead the reader through a clear line of argument and also show that you are being analytical rather than just describing or telling a story. Different types of question suggest different ways to organize and structure your argument.

'Why...?' or explanation essays

To ensure that you use an analytical approach, you could approach the essay in several ways.

- Consider long-term reasons, short-term reasons and then the trigger and use these as a structure.
- Prioritize the reasons, for example start with what you consider the most important reasons and then go on to look at other factors.
- Take a thematic approach and look at economic, social and political reasons.

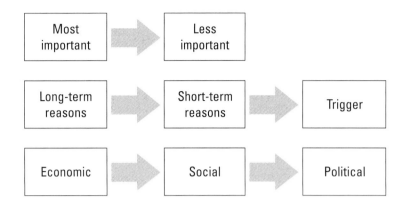

Examiner's hint

Avoid a purely chronological approach as this will lead you away from an analytical account and into more of a narrative or 'story-telling' approach. However, examiners are also looking for a 'sense of chronology' – so make sure you include dates where appropriate and deal with events in the correct order within your line of argument.

'How far…?' or 'To what extent…?' essays

Here, you need to present one side of the argument first and then give the other side of the argument. You should always start with the side that is presented in the question.

For example, for the question 'To what extent was the Tet Offensive a turning point in the Vietnam War?', start by explaining why it can be seen as a turning point and then present the alternative side of the argument.

You will need to reach a judgment as to which side you agree with the most; this should be stated in your introduction when you give your overall argument and then restated in your conclusion.

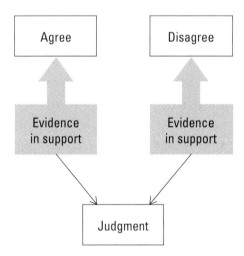

Comparative essays

Whenever you are comparing, for example, two people, wars or factors, make sure that you do this **throughout** your essay. Avoid writing about each factor separately and then having a paragraph at the end summarizing the comparisons. For example, if you are comparing Malcolm X and Dr Martin Luther King (see question 7 on page 60), make sure you make comparisons between the two men in each paragraph.

You may want to have similarities and differences on a particular point in each paragraph or you may want to deal first with similarities and then with differences.

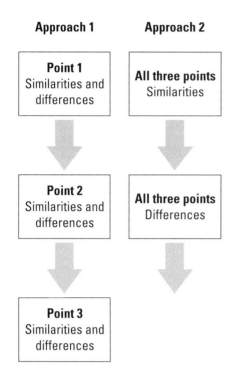

Approach 1 | Approach 2

Point 1
Similarities and differences

All three points
Similarities

Point 2
Similarities and differences

All three points
Differences

Point 3
Similarities and differences

Use of historiography

Part of your evidence may include the views of historians or even direct quotes from historians. It is good to show knowledge of historical debate. However, you must ensure that your essay is not an essay **about** historians' views; your aim is to use historical debate as evidence for your **own** argument.

Don't use quotations just to try to create the impression that you know more than you do! As with any piece of evidence, they must be selected carefully and should support the key point in the paragraph. Also, do not overdo your use of quotations – aim for one or two well-chosen, brief quotations for each key argument in your essay.

It is also worth pointing out that it is possible to meet the criteria of the higher levels without referring directly to historians. This is made clear in the History subject report (May 2010): 'Historiography should not be a substitute/replacement for solid factual knowledge, accurate chronology and sequencing which must form the basis of any effective essay.'

Activity

Read the two paragraphs below which were taken from two students' answers to the essay question: **To what extent was Stalin responsible for the purges?**

1   What is the difference in the way that each student has used historiography in his or her paragraphs?
2   Based on the quote from the subject report above, which paragraph would an IB examiner prefer to see in an essay?

> **Student A's paragraph**
>
> Although it is clear that Stalin had many motives for carrying out the purges, there are other factors that also help to explain the devastating scope of the mass killing. One of these factors is the difficulty faced by the central government of getting regional party bosses to carry out their demands. Quite often, local parties were unwilling to hunt down kulaks or to arrest specialists in industry. Thus party leaders encouraged the lower levels of the party to criticize their superiors. This meant that accusations and the terror tended to get out of control. Figes talks of a terror which 'erupted from below'.

Some do's and don'ts of essay writing

- Avoid using the first person. Although you are using your personal judgment, this should be based on an objective examination of the evidence. Using expressions such as 'I think…' do not give the impression that you are being objective.
- Make sure that you have the correct spellings for key historical figures, events and concepts.
- Use appropriate historical vocabulary. Avoid colloquial language or slang.
- Use dates to show that you understand the chronology of the events you are discussing.

- Only use official abbreviations. While abbreviations are useful when writing notes, an essay is a formal piece of writing and so all words must be written in full – 'Br.' for Britain or 'FR' for French Revolution are not acceptable.
- Don't end a sentence with 'etc.' or 'and so on'. It sends a clear message that you have run out of ideas or that you cannot be bothered to write down more points.
- Be careful with your use of metaphors. While these can add colour to your writing and illuminate certain points or ideas, they can also detract from your key argument and end up being confusing or inaccurate.

The following table gives useful phrases to use when essay writing.

To discuss a sequence of events or points	To emphasize a point	To add information
First(ly), Second(ly), Third(ly), Finally,	Moreover, Significantly, Another key point is… Surprisingly, On the negative side, On the positive side, In fact, It is important to realize… Indeed,	Additionally, In addition, Moreover, Equally important is… Furthermore, Likewise, For example, Another point/piece of evidence is…
To make a contrasting point	**To make a similar point or to compare**	**To conclude or summarize**
Although Conversely, In spite of this, On the other hand, However, On the contrary,	Similarly, Likewise,	As a result, Consequently, Accordingly, Thus, Therefore, In conclusion, To conclude,

The conclusion

As the final paragraph of your essay and the last bit that your teacher or examiner will read, it is important that your conclusion leaves a good impression. Try to make enough time in an examination to reach your conclusion as it gives you the chance to remind the reader of your argument.

In your conclusion it is important to:

- restate your main point or argument
- link back to the title to show that your argument answers the question set.

Don't introduce any new points or evidence in your conclusion.

Activity

Assess the impact of nuclear weapons on the nature and development of the Cold War.

Below you will find:

- the main points that answer this question
- the evidence that supports these points.

Work in pairs on the following tasks.

- Decide which are the main points. These will become your opening sentences to each paragraph. You may find it helpful to copy the main points onto strips of paper which you can then move around easily when deciding their order.
- Decide which supporting points go with each main point. These will provide the evidence for the rest of the paragraph.
- Decide in which order you will put your main points.
- Write an introduction and a conclusion to this essay.

Both sides raced to keep up with each other in both the development and the quantity of nuclear weapons. Thus the hydrogen bomb followed the atomic bomb in the 1950s. These were followed by inter-continental ballistic missiles, anti-ballistic missiles and multiple independently targetable re-entry vehicles.

Ultimately, the cost of nuclear weapons for the Soviet Union was to contribute to its economic decay and eventual collapse, and thus the ending of the Cold War.

The existence of nuclear weapons led to a nuclear arms race which was a dominant feature of the Cold War from 1949 until 1987.

The focus on the arms race and of nuclear weapons as the key measurement of strength for a superpower disguised the fact that the Soviet Union was economically weak.

Nuclear weapons had a key impact on the development of military strategy as both sides tried to work out how nuclear weapons could best be used.

Although both sides realized that nuclear weapons could not realistically be used without the destruction of the world, it was still essential for each side to have as many weapons as possible to prevent the other side from attacking. This led to both sides accumulating thousands of nuclear weapons by the end of the 1960s – enough to destroy the world several times over.

In the Korean War, the USSR made sure that it took no direct role. The US government also avoided widening the war and resisted calls from General MacArthur to use nuclear weapons against China.

By the mid-1980s, the Soviet Union was spending between 15 and 17 per cent of its annual gross domestic product on military spending.

Firstly, in the 1950s, Eisenhower came up with the military strategy of 'massive retaliation' by which the United States aimed to use all its weapons against the Communist world in a conflict.

Gaddis argues that the development of the strategy of Mutually Assured Destruction (MAD) meant that 'destruction was exchanged for duration' as both sides sought to avoid a nuclear show down.

The danger of nuclear weapons being used in a conflict led both sides to avoiding head-on confrontations during the Cold War. It forced them to take measures to ensure that wars did not escalate.

Wars were fought 'by proxy', i.e. via guerrilla groups or other governments.

However, the Cuban Missile Crisis showed the danger of any strategy that attempted to use nuclear weapons in a 'limited' way. By the 1960s, and after the dangers of using nuclear weapons was made clear by the Cuban Missile Crisis, MAD became the accepted strategy for both sides – i.e. an acceptance that using nuclear weapons would lead to mutual destruction. MAD became the policy of deterrence and lasted until the mid-1980s.

In incidents such as the Hungarian Uprising, Eisenhower was careful to make it clear that he would not intervene so as to avoid triggering any defensive action on the part of the Soviets.

This was followed by an alternative strategy, that of 'counterforce'. This was put forward by McNamara; it aimed to use nuclear weapons in a 'limited' way against military installations only.

The cost of developing and building up stockpiles of nuclear weapons led to a huge economic drain for both countries and this was to have an impact on both the development of the Cold War and the reasons for why it ended.

Writing essays in the examination

Paper 2

For Paper 2, you have to answer two essay questions, taken from two different topics. You will have 45 minutes for each essay.

Within each topic, there will be a total of six questions:

- three questions on named people, themes, topics or events that are listed in the syllabus
- two open-ended questions for which you can choose your own examples
- at least one question that addresses social, economic or gender issues
- at least one of the above types of question that will expect you to use material from two different regions (there will be a map on the front of the paper to remind you of the regions).

Any one of these questions could be a comparative question or based on a quotation.

Paper 3

In Paper 3, you will have to answer any three essay questions out of the 24. There will be two questions on each section of the syllabus.

You will have 50 minutes for each essay.

Expectations for SL essays and HL essays

The *IB Diploma Programme History guide* makes this distinction between expectations for SL and HL students:

'While many of the skills of studying history are common to both SL and HL, the HL student is required, through in-depth study, to synthesize and critically evaluate knowledge. The greater depth of study required for HL, and the greater demands this makes of the student, are exemplified through the nature of the learning outcomes for the HL options.… In HL Paper 3, the emphasis is on testing assessment objective 3: synthesis and evaluation, reflected in the markband descriptors.'

from *IB History guide,* © International Baccalaureate 2008

In Paper 3 essays you therefore need to show an in-depth knowledge of the region that you have studied and an understanding of historical processes.

Hints for the examination

The essay-writing skills that you have developed over the previous two years will all help you in the examination. Essay planning and revision skills (see chapter 6) will help you to enter the examination with confidence. Here are some tips to think about.

- Enter the examination prepared; make sure you know exactly what content you should know for each paper and – for Paper 2 – which topics you are focusing on.
- Take a few minutes to read the questions and make a decision as to which ones you are going to answer. Do not be tempted by questions that you have not directly studied in class.
- Read the questions carefully; misinterpreting the question is a common error – use your skills of question analysis as explained on pages 60–61 to help you work out exactly what is required for each question.

- In the examination, you should allow about 5 minutes for planning your essay before you start writing. This is key for the reasons already explained on page 62. You will be able to refer back to your plan. It will also show the examiner that you thought about your argument before writing. Put a line through the plan to indicate that it is not part of the answer.
- Be strict with your timing. Do not run over on the first essay and then run out of time for the next essay. However good your first essay is, it will not compensate for half of a second essay.

Do not waste time writing out the question.

Examiner's hint

Don't learn essays by rote. Each examination question is different and your rote answer will rarely fit the exact question that has been set.

Activity

Read the essays on the next few pages. As you read, identify and highlight examples where the student has done the following:

Introduction	• shown an understanding of the demands of the question • set out his or her argument.
Structure of paragraphs	• provided 'signpost' sentences linking to the question and setting out an argument • given appropriate evidence which supports the argument or claim set out in the opening sentence • made links between paragraphs.
Content	• shown a sense of chronology • shown a detailed knowledge of the period • indicated an understanding of historical debate • used historians as evidence to support his or her argument.
Language	• used appropriate historical terminology.
Conclusion	• linked back to the question and answered it.

Essay 1 (Paper 2)

To what extent did the Cold War between the USA and the USSR become less confrontational between 1970 and 1980?

The 1960s were very confrontational for the participants of the Cold War, the USA and USSR, with the Berlin Crisis of 1961 and the Cuban Missile crisis of 1962, an intense arms race and the practice of brinkmanship. A period of detente after 1970 was thus a welcome change between the USSR, the USA and also China. This period in the Cold War marked a change of strategy between the two superpowers in their methods of dealing with one another; the new cooperation in certain areas was designed to improve relations and thus lower the risk of confrontation. However, an undercurrent of difficulties between the superpowers continued to antagonize relations and these exploded into outright hostility in 1979 thus re-establishing a confrontational situation by 1979.

The decade of detente can be seen as making the Cold War less confrontational in the area of nuclear weapons. Following the Cuban Missile Crisis, the superpowers came to understand that mutually assured destruction (MAD) was a very real possibility. This helped to pave the way for several key arms control agreements. The most important of these was SALT I. This treaty covered areas such as the limit and location of ABMs, ICBMs and SLBMs. It also put down rules for the conduct of nuclear war and the development of weapons. As John Mason said, SALT I was able to start 'a process of institutionalised arms control'. It helped to reduce tension and thus the possibility of a nuclear confrontation between the two nuclear powers.

Agreements such as SALT I paved the way for agreements and negotiations in other areas of the Cold War which were to further reduce confrontation. One of these was improved East-West relations in Europe. This was known as 'Ostpolitik' and was advanced by Willy Brandt, Chancellor of West Germany. The Final Quadripartite protocol of 1972 was a major victory for Ostpolitik as it confirmed that West Germany had a legal basis for access routes to the West. This ensured that the situation in Germany was less likely to result in a war between the superpowers. East and West Germany also signed the Basic Treaty of 1972. This accepted the existence of two Germanys, consequently improving trade links between the two countries and reducing tension and confrontation in Europe.

The agreements in Europe became part of the Helsinki Agreement, which was the 'high point' in cooperation during this period as 33 countries were able to work together to decide on a comprehensive agreement. Firstly, following the Ostpolitik negotiations it was agreed that Europe's new frontiers were to be 'inviolable'. Secondly, a cooperation basket called for closer collaboration in economic, scientific and cultural fields. Finally, the third basket supported the protection of human rights and individual freedoms. Although this last basket was one of controversy for the USSR, all countries supported this agreement, indicating that this was a period of cooperation rather than confrontation.

However, despite this outward show of cooperation, there were several areas of confrontation that still existed after 1970. Key to this situation is the fact that attitudes between the superpowers had not really changed. Fundamentally, they were still as suspicious of each other's ideological differences meaning that detente would never allow total cooperation between the two powers. Increasingly, many Americans also came to see detente as a 'trick' (Richard Pipes) from the Soviets whereby they were using the show of cooperation as a cover for expansionism. Thus there are still several situations during the 1970s that point to a notable level of Cold War tension which was to lead to confrontation.

Firstly, detente came under pressure due to the fact that the USA felt that the arms agreements were benefiting the Soviet Union only. They worried that the Soviets were building strategic superiority through its ICBMs. Secondly, the USA could see the Soviet Union strengthening its influence in the Middle East – through giving weapons and aid to Arab states – and in Africa. Here the USSR supported the MPLA in the civil war of Angola and then, in 1977, assisted Ethiopia against Somalia. This scale of intervention suggested to the USA that the Soviets were expanding in key areas and this laid the foundation for serious confrontation by the end of the decade.

This growing distrust of the Soviets by the USA was increased by the USSR's blatant disregard of the human rights basket of the Helsinki Agreement. The Soviets had believed that they could sign the Helsinki Agreement and then ignore the commitment to human rights that the agreement entailed. However, the Carter administration became increasingly determined to link any trade deals with the Soviets to 'good behaviour' in the area of human rights. For example, the USA wanted Soviet Jews to be able to emigrate in return for improved trading conditions.

Consequently, by the late 1970s, 'the complexities and contradictions of detente had become explosive' (Fitzgerald) and when the Soviets invaded Afghanistan, cooperation between the USA and the USSR ended. The USA believed that this was another example of Soviet expansion and a threat to world peace. From this point on, confrontation escalated between the superpowers. Carter refused to approve SALT II and stopped US athletes from participating in the 1980 Olympics. He promised to increase defence spending and issued the Carter Doctrine.

To conclude, it can be argued that there was a considerable reduction in confrontation between the superpowers in the decade after 1970. The policies of detente tackled the risk of MAD through arms agreements and Ostpolitik reduced tension in Europe. All of this made confrontation much less likely. However, the undercurrent of suspicion and tension between the superpowers during the years 1970 to 1980 cannot be ignored as these lay the foundation for an intensification of confrontation after the collapse of detente in 1979.

Essay 2 (Paper 3)

'He brought his country and his people nothing but harm.' To what extent do you agree with this assessment of Stalin's domestic policies in the USSR between 1929 and 1953?

© IB Organization 2004

After emerging successful in the power struggle in 1929, Stalin, over the next 24 years, carried out several key policies which were to transform the Soviet Union; collectivization, the five-year plans, the great purges, along with an expansion of the cult of personality, increased propaganda and censorship. These domestic policies caused extreme harm to both his people and his country. However, despite the immense human suffering, some aspects of these policies can also be seen as successful for the USSR as a whole. The economic policies turned the USSR into an industrialized nation, allowing it to survive the German onslaught in the Second World War and laying the foundations for it becoming a superpower after 1945.

Stalin's policy of collectivization can be seen to have caused nothing but harm to his people and to the Soviet Union. Firstly, Stalin's main push of collectivization from 1929 to 1941 resulted in up to 14.5 million kulaks being killed, and caused a massive famine in the Ukraine from 1932–1933, causing 3–5 million people to starve. Grain output dropped from 73 million tons in 1928 to 68 million tons in 1933, while the number of farm animals also dropped dramatically due to the peasants burning crops and slaughtering their animals rather than handing them over to the collective farms. Even though less grain was produced, Stalin took more of it to give it to the cities, which contained only around 20% of the Soviet Union's population and this suggests Stalin allowed his people to starve, thus causing nothing but harm to his people.

Economically, collectivization was also a disaster for the Soviet Union. Grain harvests dropped dramatically in the early 1930s and did not recover to their 1928 level until the end of the 1930s. Russia also did not recover from its loss of animals until after the Second World War. Thus Stalin's forced rapid collectivization resulted in the stagnation of Russia's agricultural economy, which would remain the Soviet Union's weakest point until its collapse.

The purges that Stalin carried out between 1936 and 1939 also brought nothing but harm to the Soviet people and the state. Around 3.5 million people were imprisoned or executed during these three years. Thus Stalin killed massive amounts of his own people often brutally, not because it helped the state or the people, but because of his paranoia that there were enemies everywhere. This suggests that Stalin was not acting in the best interests of the state or his people, but just to satisfy his paranoia and to maintain his despotic hold of the Soviet Union.

The purges weakened many areas of society, but one of the most important areas that was weakened was the military. Stalin killed most of the Soviet Union's most educated and intelligent army officers and generals. Moshe Lewin describes the purges as destroying its 'backbone and brain' – 80% of colonels, all admirals and their replacements were killed and 90% of all generals were killed. This left the Russian military exhausted and unable to fight. Thus in the Winter War of 1939 to 1940, when Russia invaded the tiny country of Finland, the Soviets lost six times as many troops as the Finns. It also left the Soviet Union weakened in the face of the Nazi invasion in 1941. This suggests that Stalin's domestic policy of the purges was detrimental to the Soviet people and state, and did nothing but harm.

Stalin's expansion of his cult of personality and censorship from 1929 to 1953 also caused harm to the Soviet Union and its people. The intense propaganda glorifying Stalin, along with the control of all history and culture, allowed no room for freedoms of any kind. Socialist realism was the only art form allowed; literary progress was stopped by Zhdanov, who imprisoned many 'anti-state' cultural icons like Anna Akhmatova. Thus Stalin hurt Russia's culture. Robert Service writes, for example, that 'No great work of literature was published in the 1930s and artistic figures went in fear of their lives.'

However, despite the horrors and harm of collectivization and the purges, there were some aspects of Stalin's domestic policies between 1929 and 1953 that did in fact bring benefits to the Soviet people. Firstly, collectivization did help the industrial development of the Soviet Union. Stalin's agricultural policies created massive migration to cities: the urban population from 1928 to 1939 increased from 26 million to 38 million, with the number employed increasing from 11 million to 26 million in the same time frame. This contributed to the massive industrialization of Russia which was to play a key part in its survival in the Second World War. Secondly, agriculture was able to grow quickly after 1945, reaching 1941 levels by 1952, indicating that by this time the collective farms were working more efficiently.

The five-year plans from 1929 to 1953, enacted by Stalin as part of his domestic policy, are possibly the best example of Stalin's domestic policies helping the Soviet Union. The first five-year plan, from 1929 to 1933, increased pig iron output from 3 million tons to 6 million tons, crude oil output from 11 million tons to 21 million tons, electricity supplied from 5 million gigavolts to 13.5 million gigavolts, and created around 50,000 new tractors for farmers to use by 1933. This meant that by 1937 the Soviet Union's steel output almost reached that of Germany's. The second and third five-year plans concentrated more on the armaments industry and by 1940 the Soviet Union was in a position to create the weaponry needed to fight Germany. In the battle of Kursk in 1942, for example, the Soviet Union was able to field 3,400 tanks in the largest tank battle in history compared to Germany's 2,400 tanks. Thus it could be argued that this industrialization allowed the Soviet Union to survive during the Second World War.

Moreover, after the war, the fourth and fifth five-year plans from 1946 to 1950 and 1951 to 1955 enriched the Soviet's heavy industry, causing steel production in 1952 to be double that of 1941, and coal production in the Donets Basin in 1952 to exceed that of 1941. Therefore, Stalin's five-year plans helped to industrialize the Soviet Union. This came at a cost to the Soviet people in terms of the working and living conditions, but it could be argued that the fact that it allowed the Soviet Union to survive the war and to rebuild after the war was ultimately a key point, which did not harm the Soviet state or people, but rather helped them.

The weight of evidence is heavily against Stalin's domestic policy being successful for his people or the state. The quality of life dropped, culture stagnated, millions died both through the purges and through a manmade famine. However, ultimately and despite the human suffering, the industrialization aspect of his domestic policy had positive rather than negative results. The Soviet Union's industry grew faster than that of any other country in the history of the world, and this contributed to the Soviets' victory in the Second World War and its emergence as a superpower after 1945.

The internal assessment: the historical investigation

"You don't have any books do you?"

How does the historical investigation fit into the IB Diploma Programme in history?

The internal assessment (IA), or historical investigation, is your opportunity to explore a period, theme or event in history that you are interested in and would enjoy investigating further. It is also an important component of your final grade: 20% for HL students and 25% for SL students. Your teacher will grade your final piece of work. However, a sample of investigations from your class will then be sent to the IB for moderation and therefore the actual grade awarded for the IA will be given to you when your final examination results are published.

In the IA you will have the opportunity to demonstrate the full range of assessment objectives:

- knowledge and understanding
- application and interpretation
- synthesis and evaluation
- document analysis.

This means that you need to start this investigation only after this range of skills has been taught and practised in class. It is also advisable that you cover a number of key themes and issues in your history course before beginning your IA and that you are familiar with historical terminology and able to use it appropriately. This could be towards the end of your first year, or during your second year.

If you are doing your IA in the second year of your course, make sure that you begin it at least three months before the deadline for submission of samples to IBCA to allow enough time to complete it.

An example of an IA time line is given below.

Time	Tasks
26 April	Select topic and gather general materials to bring to class for 6 May.
6 May	Initial research and refinement of question. Begin section A, section B and bibliography.
17 May	First draft of section A, section B and bibliography submitted.
20 May	First draft of sections C–F submitted.
27 May	Final draft of IA submitted. TWO hard copies and ONE electronic copy to the teacher via a plagiarism-checking website.

You are expected to spend approximately 20 hours researching your topic, refining your question and writing up the investigation. The final written product must be between 1,500 and 2,000 words. This does not include references, headings, subheadings or section F (your list of works cited).

What can you write about in the IA?

The IA should be an extension of your knowledge and understanding of history. It can be related to a topic studied in class, but it could also be a topic that you have not covered in your IB history course. Choosing a topic and then refining it into a research question is one of the hardest tasks of the IA. Remember these points:

- It should be a topic that you are genuinely interested in.
- It can be on any topic but you need to be able to access, read, analyse and evaluate a wide range of sources, including primary and secondary sources where possible.
- It can involve any time period except the last ten years, due to the fact that objective sources would be limited within this time frame.
- You need to be able to put the topic into its historical context and reflect on its significance so choosing a topic from an era of history that you know little about could be a problem.
- It could include reference to historical literature, films or documentaries.

Once you have chosen your topic, you need to narrow it down to a specific research question which will allow you to take an analytical approach. Here is an example.

Topic: Solidarity in Poland

could be refined to:

Working title: To what extent was the success of Solidarity due to Lech Walesa?

Your question will generally be worded in a similar style to those on Papers 2 and 3. However, it needs to be more specific and focused than a general essay examination question.

Activity

Read through the following possible historical investigation titles.

- which of the titles are suitable questions for historical investigations
- which ones need development and refinement; how could these be worked into suitable IA questions?

In pairs, decide:

- which of the titles are suitable questions for historical investigations
- which ones need development and refinement; how could these be worked into suitable IA questions?

1 The Algerian War

2 To what extent did economic problems lead to the military coup d'état against King Idris of Libya on 1 September 1969?

3 Germany's involvement in the Spanish Civil War between 1936–1939

4 The impact of the Suez Crisis on Britain

5 To what extent was the Japanese occupation of Indonesia a key factor in its gaining independence in December 1949?

6 Was the CIA responsible for the overthrow of Salvador Allende's government in 1973?

7 To what extent was the French decision to occupy the Ruhr on 11 January 1923 attributable to Germany's failure to pay reparations?

8 Did the Abyssinian Crisis (1935–36) harm Mussolini's Italy?

9 Cuba's involvement in the Angolan Civil War

10 To what extent was Kennedy a bad president?

11 To what extent was the General Strike of 1926 caused by conditions in the mining industry?

12 Who was Tito and what was his legacy for Yugoslavia?

13 Why did Solidarity win the elections of 1989 in Poland?

14 To what extent can General Franco's Nationalists be held responsible for the bombing of Guernica on 26 April 1937?

15 Why did the Soviet Union invade Czechoslovakia?

16 The UN's failure to respond to the genocide in Rwanda

17 What was the impact of the 1980 Olympic boycott?

18 Why did Oswald Mosley leave the Labour Party to form the British Union of Fascists?

19 To what extent was neutrality broken by Switzerland in the Second World War?

20 Why did American-mediated negotiations supporting the formation of a CCP-GMD coalition government in China from 1944–1947 fail?

21 Japan's post-war economic recovery

22 To what extent was Churchill's victory in the 1952 general election due to the Labour Party's mismanagement of the post-war economy?

23 Mao and propaganda

24 PoWs and the Korean War

25 How useful is Ken Loach's film Land and Freedom for investigating the role of foreign intervention in the Spanish Civil War?

26 Religious beliefs in pre-Islamic Arabia

27 How successful was the medieval rule of Matilda (1102–67)?

28 Civil wars (fitna) in early Islamic history, 656–61

How should you go about collecting evidence?

After you have devised a working question, you need to begin your research.

■ You should aim to have a variety of sources including secondary and primary sources where possible. We would recommend that you use no less than eight sources for a research work of this length at diploma level.

■ For primary sources, consider not only newspapers and journals from the time, but also public broadcasts and published diaries, government papers and speeches (which are often available online, for example *Hansard* is the minutes from British parliamentary debates). You can also include personal interviews with family, friends or other relevant figures to your investigation.

- Refer to pages 16–20 for ideas on secondary sources. Historians are a key source as you should be researching a topic that has generated work by reputable historians.
- Read widely around the topic starting with the more general texts first and then moving to the specific, as outlined on page 7.
- Take care to note down your resources as you use them. See pages 9–16 for suggestions on how to take notes.
- As you gather your evidence you might need to adjust your question. For example, if you have the working title: To what extent did the religious policies of X lead to her fall from power in …? and in your research there is very little evidence of religious policies affecting events but much evidence and debate surrounding the role of economic policies and foreign policy, you might change the focus of your question to bring it in line with the evidence. Your new question would be: To what extent did the economic and foreign policies of X lead to her fall from power in…?

In order to identify causes, effects or turning points, it is sometimes useful to draft a time line of key dates before and after your chosen 'event'. After sorting your material chronologically, you can then begin to sort your evidence **thematically**. Try to include not only the significant dates, events and supporting data, but different contemporary opinions as well as historians' viewpoints.

Tip

Remember to look for online government documents, including minutes of parliamentary debates, declassified documents, etc.

If your IA is based on a field trip or heritage site you might be able to generate your own sources.

Remember that if you conduct your own interview you need to include a transcript of it in an appendix.

Activity

The following set of notes comes from a student who is writing an essay on the role of the Yalta Conference in causing the breakdown of the Grand Alliance. Study them carefully and then answer the following questions.

1 What themes has the student identified as significant for her research?

2 What else is significant abut the way she has organized her notes?

3 Refer to the section on note taking on pages 9–16. What other methods could she have used to collect and make notes on this information?

4 Why has she included page references with the key bits of information and with the quotes?

Crockatt, R., 1994, *The Fifty Years War*, London: Routledge.

Overall situation

The US and the USSR had little in common prior to the war and ending of Germany as an enemy 'exposed the largely utilitarian purpose which had led to the formation of the Alliance' (pg. 46).

Germany

The US realized that an impoverished and resentful Germany would cause instability in Europe (pg. 53).

The issue of joint control was an area of dispute (pg. 54).

Poland

The dispute over boundaries was solved by 'Stalin's fait accompli' (pg. 52) by which the border was moved westwards some 150 miles.

The Soviet Union made it clear that it was unprepared to accord the non-communists any real role or to conduct the kind of elections that would satisfy the West (pg. 53).

Judt, T., 2005, *Postwar: A History of Europe since 1945*, London: Penguin.

Overall situation

'Four years of wary cooperation… had done little to obliterate nearly thirty years of mutual suspicion' (pg. 103).

Germany

The issue of Germany was left off the table as 'it was so intractable' (pg. 102).

Eastern Europe

By this time 'Stalin hardly needed Western permission to do what ever he wished in Eastern Europe' (pg. 102).

Stalin said of the Declaration on Liberated Europe, 'We can fulfil it in our own way. What matters is the correlation of forces' (pg. 103).

Barras, G., 2009, *The Great Cold War, A Journey Through the Hall of Mirrors*, Stanford, CA: Stanford University Press.

Overall situation

Stalin was interested that Roosevelt was talking of removing troops from Europe as soon as he could as this would allow the Soviet Union to become the main power on the continent; this would make it more likely that other countries would become communist (pg. 29).

Poland

'A clash between the big three over Poland was inevitable' (pg. 30).

Roosevelt and Churchill were both committed to the Poles and the Poles had also given great help to the allied war effort, e.g. intelligence. The Polish government in exile in London was very suspicious of Stalin especially after the Katyn Forest massacre. Stalin resented Western attempts to influence a Polish government as he was adamant it should be friendly to the USSR.

Activity

Use a sheet like the one below to do your initial planning. Check it with your teacher to see if your question and sources are appropriate.

IA PLANNING SHEET	
NAME:	
TOPIC:	
RESEARCH QUESTION:	
Primary sources	
Secondary sources	
Online resources	

Which two sources do you plan to evaluate in section C?

1 _____

2 _____

Using the assessment criteria

There are six sections to your IA. You must produce a written account consisting of each of the six sections outlined below. Use each of the sections A–F as clear subheadings in your final written investigation.

Section A: Plan of the investigation

This is worth 3 marks. To get these 3 marks you need to do the following.

- State your **research question**. You could briefly explain reasons for choosing your theme though this is not essential. For example, the title 'To what extent was the success of Solidarity due to Lech Walesa?' could include the following: 'I chose this topic because, coming from Poland, I was intrigued to investigate the reasons for the dramatic changes that took place in my country in 1989.'
- Define the **scope** of the investigation. This means clearly identifying the themes or lines of argument considered in your research, for example: 'As well as the role of Lech Walesa, other factors such as the influence of the Catholic Church, the situation inside the Soviet Union and the economic crisis in Poland will be analysed as to their impact on the situation in 1989.' You should also set down a time frame, for example 'the years 1980 to 1989 will be the focus of this investigation'.
- Explain the **method** used: that is, what types of sources will be used, and which two key sources you will be evaluating and why: 'A range of both Polish and Western sources have been used. A thorough evaluation has been done of a poster used by Lech Walesa to increase his votes in the election, and of an extract from a British book written before the collapse of the Soviet Union. These sources give contrasting reasons concerning the impact of Lech Walesa.'

Examiner's hints

Make sure that the research question is included in section A as no credit can be given for a question that only appears on the cover sheet or as a title.

For the scope of the investigation it is not necessary to state what has not been included.

The suggested word count for this section is 100–150 words.

Activity

Read the sample plan below for section A. Highlight in different colours where these different elements have been included:

- research question
- scope
- methods used.

> **Example section A: Plan of the investigation**
>
> This investigation will explore the question: To what extent was the General Strike of 1926 caused by conditions in the mining industry? The scope of my research will assess whether these conditions were the primary reasons for the strike in May 1926, or whether it was broader economic and political problems that led to this strike. The breadth of research is the years 1914–1926.
>
> The method used will be to gather a range of evidence from primary and secondary sources, compare and contrast this evidence, as well as evaluate the origin and purpose of my sources for their values and limitations. Two sources – the essay 'British Imperialism and the Labour Aristocracy' by John Foster and the Cabinet Conclusions, 6 October 1921 – will be evaluated in depth as they provide significant and conflicting evidence. Finally, based upon the weight of evidence and source evaluations, a conclusion will be reached.

Section B: A summary of evidence

The key to this section is to set down your evidence clearly, and ensure that you have consistently referenced the material. Your summary of evidence must be organized, usually thematically, and it must show that you have conducted a thorough piece of research. It can be presented as either a numbered or point list, or as continuous prose and is worth 6 marks. An example showing evidence given as a numbered list follows.

Example list section B: A summary of evidence

1   Conditions in the mining industry

a   70% of mine owners' costs were for labour – wages would be cut.[1]

b   'Miners were among the nation's worst paid workers and suffered the nation's highest rate of unemployment.'[2]

c   Wages dropped 26% from 1920–1924.[3]

d   'After 1918 the export market collapsed leaving the industry with around a quarter to a third surplus capacity.'[4]

e   The industry was affected by Treaty of Versailles: Germany would 'supply free reparations coal to her former enemies, Italy and France'.[5]

f   In the 1920s, demand for coal decreased and the use of oil as a substitute increased, e.g. fuel in British ships.[6]

g   'Between 1922 and 1924, 3,603 miners were killed and 597,158 injured.'[7]

h   By mid-1925, the 'industry was losing £1 million a month, while… more than a tenth of the total [collieries were] forced to close.'[8]

i   In 1925, the miners' working day lengthened from 7 to 8 hours, and pay was reduced by 13–38%.[9]

j   '[The strike] was called by a reluctant, apprehensive Trades Union Congress to defend the living standards of… the miners.'[10]

k   Trigger: the Samuel Commission issued in March 1926 would end the government subsidy of £25 million and bring further pay-cuts – this led to a lock-out (1 April 1926).[11]

2   Broader economic problems

a   The Triple Alliance was formed in April 1914 (comprising 1.5 million miners, railwaymen and transport workers) after a period of strikes.[12]

b   'The war led to over-investment in… iron, steel, coal, shipbuilding and textiles [which] were not needed in such quantities in peacetime.'[13]

c   'Inter-war depression' saw 'mass-unemployment', 'industrial unrest' and the collapse of industry.[14]

---

1 Pugh, M., 'The General Strike: On the 80th anniversary of the General Strike, Martin Pugh revisits one of the most bitter disputes in history and assesses its impact on industrial relations and the wider political landscape of the twentieth century.' *History Today*, 13 May 2010, pp. 13–16.

2 'Great Britain's General Strike, 1926', *Discovering World History*. Online edn. accessed 13 May 2010.

3 Foster, J., 1976, *The General Strike 1926*, London: Lawrence and Wishart, pg. 13.

4 Pugh, M., *op. cit.*

5 Phillips, G. A., 1976, *The General Strike: the Politics of Industrial Conflict*, London: Weidenfield and Nicolson, pg. 25.

6 Phillips, G. A., *op. cit.*, pg. 25.

7 Rees, R., 2003, *The General Strike of 1926: Revolution or muddle? Britain 1890-1939*, Oxford: Heinemann, pg. 124.

8 Renshaw, P., *op. cit.*, pg. 118.

9 Rees, R., *op. cit.*, pg. 124.

10 Foster, J., *op. cit.*, pg. 3.

11 Stanton, P., 2000, *Britain 1919–29: Post-war Prosperity? A case study of the General Strike, Britain 1905–1951*, Cheltenham: Stanley Thornes, pp. 15–16. Google Books. Accessed 27 May 2010.

12 Renshaw, P., *op. cit.*, pg. 47.

13 Rees, R., *op. cit.*, pg. 117.

14 Renshaw, P., *op. cit.*, pg. 56.

d 'By 1919 USA was producing two-thirds of the world's steel' and European economic collapse hindered Britain.[15]

e 'Three-quarters of the jobless [in 1920–21] were in… shipbuilding, textile manufacture, engineering and coal mining, [where] 20–30% were permanently unemployed.'[16]

f 1921: 'Prime Minister described [unemployment] as unprecedented' as a large number of the unemployed were skilled workers.[17]

g The government put Britain back on the gold standard in 1925; prices of exports rose by 10% – less foreign trade.[18]

h The pound was overvalued by 2.5–10%.[19]

i Imports increased 10% from 1913–1925 while exports decreased 25%.[20]

3 Political discontent

a In 1920, of the 288 Trades and Labour Councils, 139 voted in favour of ending the economic blockade of the USSR 'in defiance of the right-wing national leadership'.[21]

b November 1924; 'the stage was set for the offensive against the conditions of the British working class. Economic crisis was to be translated into political attack.'[22]

c Trotsky's book *Whither England (1925)* – 'gradual and painless penetration of communism into the ranks of the British Labour Party and trade unions'.[23]

d Fear of communism (from the 1917 Bolshevik revolution) in Britain exacerbated problems with Trade Unionism; forgery of the Zinoviev Letter (1924).[24]

e Zinoviev Letter, addressed to the British Communist Party published in the *Daily Mail:* 'It is indispensable to stir up the masses of the British proletariat' to 'bring increased pressure to bear upon the Government'.[25]

f *Daily Mail* dispute (3 May 1926): Printers refused to print a passage including: 'The General Strike is… a revolutionary movement, intended to inflict suffering on the great mass of innocent persons.'[26]

g *British Gazette*, 6 May 1926: 'The General Strike is in operation, expressing in no uncertain terms a direct challenge to ordered government.'[27]

15 Foster, J., *op. cit.*, pg. 8.

16 Renshaw, P., *op. cit.*, pg. 91.

17 Cabinet Conclusions. The National Archives, 6 October 1921. Accessed 19 May 2010. http://filestore.nationalarchives.gov.uk/pdfs/small/cab-23-27-cc-76-21-3.pdf

18 Rees, R., *op. cit.*, pg. 124.

19 Renshaw, P., *op. cit.*, pg. 117.

20 Renshaw, P., *ibid.*, pg. 90.

21 Foster, J., *op. cit.*, pg. 28.

22 Kluggman, J, 1976, *The General Strike 1926*, London: Lawrence and Wishart, pg. 58.

23 Marsden, C., 'Stalin, Trotsky and the 1926 British General Strike', Accessed 10 May 2010. http://www.wsws.org/articles/2008/dec2008/bgnl-d27.shtml

24 Pugh, M., *op. cit.*

25 'The Zinoviev Letter' 15 September 1924, *Text of the 'Zinoviev Letter' as received by SIS on 8 October 1924*, 93–95, The National Archives. Accessed 19 May 2010. http://collections.europarchive.org/tna/20080205132101/fco.gov.uk/files/kfile/92e86b92fzinoviev-2fannexa,0.pdf

26 Rees, R., *op. cit.*, pg. 131.

27 Chapman, P., 'General Strike 1926: Revolutionary action or act of desperation?', *Hindsight*, pp 13–15, May 2010.

Tip

Don't forget that for this section you are expected to have:

- factual material drawn from sources appropriate to the investigation; sources should be sufficient to provide in-depth understanding of the topic and be specifically relevant to the question
- correct and consistent referencing which must conform to a standard acceptable system (see pages 91–94 on how to do this)
- organization of the points made – either thematically or chronologically

Examiner's hints

Section B should not include any **analysis** of your evidence.

The suggested word count for this section is 500–600 words and you should err towards the upper word limit to achieve the full 6 marks.

Activity

Look at the bullet points of evidence in the example section B list above.

1 How has the evidence been organized? Can you think of other headings under which the evidence could be organized?

2 Roughly how many sources have been used as evidence?

3 What different types of sources have been used?

4 What would be the advantages and the disadvantages of writing the same information as prose?

5 Look at the assessment criteria for section B on page 82. How many marks would you give this example?

Section C: An evaluation of sources

This section is worth 5 marks. To get these marks you need to:

- critically evaluate **two** important sources appropriate to the investigation
- refer explicitly to the origin, purpose, value and limitation of the selected sources.

Your choice of sources is important. They must be sources that you can use meaningfully in your investigation and should not, for example, include a textbook or encyclopaedia or general website. They should appear in your evidence in section B (referenced) and again in your analysis in section D.

You must focus on the **origin and purpose** of each source – not on the content of the source. You can write about each source separately, or you can discuss both as a running commentary. We recommend the first option, so that your treatment of each source is clear and thorough.

Example section C: An evaluation of sources

Foster, J. (1976) 'British Imperialism and the Labour aristocracy' in Skelley, J. *The General Strike, 1926,* London: Lawrence and Wishart, pp. 3–57.

The origin of the source is of value because the author is a professional expert in the field of history, studying at St Catherine's College, Cambridge, and lecturing in politics at Strathclyde University. He was awarded a PhD 'for a thesis on working-class consciousness in the early nineteenth century'[1], showing he is a peer-assessed professional in early 20th-century British history and politics. The essay is part of J. Skelley's book *The General Strike, 1926,* which is a collaboration of historical essays, including bibliographical information throughout.

The purpose of Foster's essay is to analyse the run-up to the General Strike of 1926. This is valuable, since it enables a variety of information to be given over a long period of time, providing academic analysis and historical evidence of the political and economic causes.

The origin of this source also limits its value, however, as Foster is a member of the Communist Party of Great Britain[2], therefore the evidence presented in the essay may not be accurate as it may focus on the trade unions and Communist Party. Also, as it was published in 1976 more evidence might since have come to light.

---

1 Skelley, J., 1976, *The General Strike, 1926,* London: Lawrence and Wishart, pp. vii–viii.

2 Skelley, J., *op. cit.,* pp. vii–viii.

The purpose of this source also makes it limited; the title, 'British Imperialism and the Labour aristocracy', uses biased language, referring to the government as 'aristocracy'. This displays Foster's political views, which are extremely left wing, and therefore the analysis may not be objective.

Cabinet Conclusions. The National Archives, 6 October 1921. Accessed 19 May 2010. http://filestore.nationalarchives.gov.uk/pdfs/small/cab-23-27-cc-76-21-3.pdf

The origin of the source is valuable since it is the minutes from a government cabinet meeting on 6 October 1921, from the British National Archives. It discusses a number of foreign and domestic issues, including unemployment and the economic situation; and contains confidential information vital to the event being researched. Present at the meeting were the prime minister, Lloyd George, and a number of other ministers who were figures of authority and would have had access to government statistics and confidential information.

The source is also valuable because its purpose is to inform a number of ministers of the foreign and domestic situation in Britain. This means that it would consist of statistics and valuable information relating to the causes of the miners' strike.

There are limitations to this source's origin. The meeting was conducted by government officials and the prime minister, therefore the information may be in line with government policy and to justify future government action. The meeting was conducted in 1921 and although it presents information about the build up to the General Strike, it does not produce evidence in the short term for why the strike occurred in 1926.

The purpose of the source is limited since the government may not have understood the miners' frustrations at the time. The purpose is to look at an overview of the situation in the country, and would not have focused specifically on coal mining.

Examiner's hint

Note that the student used the word 'biased' to explain the language of the source. Be careful with this word. Students often use it to describe a source without actually explaining **why** the source is biased and why this is relevant to their analysis. It is not enough to say a source is biased without giving a clear explanation why. Here the student has clearly explained by giving the example of use of the word 'aristocracy' and has indicated why this might be a limitation.

Examiner's hint

You must include the complete details of the source being evaluated – that is, the full provenance of the source. You will need to evaluate each part of the provenance, for example author, date of publication and place of origin. Your teacher, and in turn the moderating examiner, will need to see the full provenance to assess your evaluation properly.

The suggested word count for this section is 250–400 words. You should err towards the upper word limit in this section to ensure that you have made a thorough evaluation of each source so that you secure the full 5 marks.

Activity

Go though the source evaluation above.

For each source indicate in the margin (using the letters 'O' 'P', 'V' and 'L') where the student has:

- referred to the origin of the source
- referred to the purpose of the source
- discussed the value of the source
- discussed the limitations of the source.

With regard to the first source, complete this table to show what points the student has made about:

- the date of the source (origin)
- the author of the source (origin)
- the nature of the source (origin)
- the author's purpose.

	Value	Limitations
Date		
Author		
Nature		
Purpose		

Section D: Analysis

This section is the 'essay part' of the investigation and is worth 6 marks. Here you will be using the evidence you provided in section B and the sources you evaluated in section C to write an analysis of your question.

This section must include the following elements.

- *An analysis of the key issues related to your question must appear.*
  As in an essay, you are writing up and analysing the lines of argument that you have found in your research. For example, let's say you are looking at the **causes** of the General Strike in Britain. You have already developed different themes in your list of evidence in section B. You now present each case or theme in turn and explain why it was a cause of the General Strike. You will also be arguing which causes were more important rather than just listing them. Refer to the language for essay writing on page 69 to help you approach each paragraph in an analytical way.
- *You must show an understanding of the issue or question in its historical context.*
  In the example here, the student puts the case study into the context of 1920s Britain and the broader context of the fear of communism prevalent at the time.
- *You must make critical use of the evidence presented in section B.*
  The evidence from section B will be synthesized into your analysis as supporting examples for each line of argument. Your critical use of this can be demonstrated by your counter-claims and counter-arguments.
- *An awareness of the **significance** of the sources used, especially those in section C, must be evident.*
  The sources used in section B – but particularly those you have chosen for evaluation in section C – should be used as evidence in this section. Usually, sources from section C will give important supporting evidence to your main lines of argument in this section, and you should include an analysis of these sources.
- *Where appropriate, there should be consideration of different interpretations.*
  There may be different interpretations of your question, for example the contemporary view of the causes of an event may differ from historians' analysis. You might find that historians offer different viewpoints. These different lines of argument should be listed in section B and incorporated into your arguments in section D.
- *You must reference all evidence used in this section.*
  As with section B, each time you include evidence you must reference it here. This should be done thoroughly and be correctly formatted. You must not refer back to references given in section B or section C. If no references are included in section D a maximum of only 2 marks can be awarded. See pages 91–94 on how to do referencing.

Example section D: Analysis

Many contemporary historians, including John Foster, believe that the General Strike was the result of problems in Britain's mining industry, and 'was called by a reluctant, apprehensive Trade Unions Congress to defend the living standards… of the miners'.[1] The inter-war period saw a dramatic collapse of the industry, as demand for coal decreased and use of other fuels increased, such as oil in

---

1 Foster, J., *op. cit.*, pg. 3.

British shipping.[2] In addition, the Treaty of Versailles negatively affected the industry, as Germany was ordered to pay reparations of coal to Italy and France; meaning the demand for British coal was almost non-existent.[3] Due to the post-war situation in Europe, there was little demand for British exports, and after 1918 the coal-mining industry was left 'with around a quarter to a third surplus capacity'.[4] This meant the owners of mines were left with little choice but to cut wages, since 70% of costs went to labour[5], and between 1920 and 1924 wages were cut by 26%.[6] However, in 1925 the industry 'was losing £1 million a month' and 'more than a tenth of [collieries were] forced to close'.[7] Miners were among the nation's lowest paid workers[8] working in appalling conditions; 'between 1922 and 1924, 3,603 miners were killed and 597,158 injured'.[9] Due to the necessary cut-backs, hours were lengthened from 7 to 8 hours, and wages cut 13–38%.[10] In March 1926 the government produced the Samuel Commission, proposing an end to mining subsidies (around £25 million) along with further pay-cuts. This led to a lock-out on 1 April, which triggered the outbreak of the General Strike on 3 May 1926.[11]

However, there were also broader economic problems during the 1920s, suggesting the causes of the General Strike were perhaps broader than historians such as John Foster suggest. Even before the First World War there was unrest in British industry. The Triple Alliance, consisting of 1.5 million miners, railwaymen and transport workers, was formed in April 1914[12] and was involved in further strikes leading up to and including the General Strike. During the war there was increased industrial production; however, afterwards there was huge over-production in 'iron and steel, coal, shipbuilding and textiles…[which were] not needed in such quantities in peacetime'[13]. Additionally, the growth of the USA, which 'was producing two-thirds of the world's steel' by 1919[14] and the economic collapse of Europe hindered Britain. This caused a fall in profits in many staple industries, causing 'mass unemployment and industrial unrest' in the 1920s;[15] a situation described by the prime minister as 'unprecedented', especially as many of those unemployed were skilled workers.[16] 'Three-quarters of the jobless [in 1920–21] were in… shipbuilding, textiles and engineering' where '20 or 30%… were permanently unemployed'[17]. These problems were exacerbated in 1925, when the government put Britain back on the Gold Standard, meaning the pound was overvalued by 2.5–10%[18] and the price of exports rose by

2 Phillips, G. A., *op. cit.*, pg 25.

3 Phillips, G. A., *op. cit.*, pg. 25.

4 Pugh, M., *op. cit.*

5 Pugh, M., *op. cit.*

6 Foster, J., *op. cit.* pg. 13.

7 Renshaw, P., *op. cit.*, pg. 118.

8 'Great Britain's General Strike, 1926', *Discovering World History*. Online edn. Accessed 13 May 2010.

9 Rees, R., *op. cit.*, pg. 124.

10 Rees, R., *op. cit.*, pg. 124.

11 Stanton, P., *op. cit.*, pg. 15.

12 Renshaw, P., *op. cit.*, pg. 47.

13 Rees, R., *op. cit.*, pg. 117.

14 Foster, J,. *op. cit.*, pg. 8.

15 Renshaw, P., *op. cit.*, pg. 56.

16 Cabinet Conclusions. The National Archives, 6 October 1921. Accessed 19 May 2010. http://filestore.nationalarchives.gov.uk/pdfs/small/cab-23-27-cc-76-21-3.pdf

17 Renshaw, P., *op. cit.*, pg. 91.

18 Renshaw, P., *op. cit.*, pg. 117.

10%, causing a decrease in foreign trade.[19] Statistics suggest that although imports rose in 1925, exports were '25% down on the 1913 figure'[20]. This meant that it was extremely difficult for export industries to recover during the early 1920s, and there was discontent among the British working class as a whole.

There are also political factors leading to the outbreak of the General Strike in 1926. Historian James Kluggman claimed that although economic problems were important, the strike saw this 'translated into political attack'[21]. The British government believed the strike was an attempt at revolution, and an article in the government publication, the *British Gazette*, stated 'The General Strike is in operation, expressing in no uncertain terms a direct challenge to ordered government.'[22] This reflected popular opinion at the time, as there was a great fear of communism after the Bolshevik revolution of 1917.[23] The trade unions also had apparent links with the Communist Party, shown in 1920, when of the 288 Trades and Labour Councils, 139 voted in favour of ending the economic blockade of the USSR, and against the right-wing governments' proposals.[24] In Trotsky's book *Whither England*, he wrote of 'a gradual and painless penetration of communism into the ranks of the British Labour Party and trade unions'[25], suggesting a link to the Soviet Union. This fear was exacerbated by the 'Zinoviev Letter' published in the *Daily Mail* in 1924, a forged letter allegedly from Comintern addressed to the CPGB.[26] This letter referred to the necessity to 'stir up the masses of the British proletariat' to 'bring increased pressure… upon the government'.[27] On 3 May 1926, the day of the outbreak of the General Strike, *Daily Mail* printers refused to print a passage calling the strike 'a revolutionary movement, intended to inflict suffering on the great mass of innocent persons'.[28]

19 Rees, R., *op. cit.* pg., 124.
20 Renshaw, P., *op.cit.*, pg. 90.
21 Kluggman, J., *op. cit.*, pg. 58.
22 Chapman, P., 'General Strike 1926: Revolutionary action or act of desperation'?, *Hindsight*, 13 May 2010.
23 Pugh, M., *op. cit.*
24 Foster, J., *op. cit.* pg. 28.
25 Marsden, C., 'Stalin, Trotsky and the 1926 British General Strike'. Accessed 10 May 2010 http://www.wsws.org/articles/2008/dec2008/bgnl-d27.shtml
26 Pugh, M., *op. cit.*
27 'The Zinoviev Letter' 15 September 1924. *Text of the 'Zinoviev Letter' as received by SIS on 8 October 1924.* 93–95. The National Archives. Accessed 19 May 2010.
28 Rees, R., *op. cit.*, pg. 131.

Examiner's hints

This section is an analysis of the evidence presented in section B – **no new evidence** should be introduced in section D.

This section should consist of 600–700 words and you should err towards the higher end of the word count to get the full 6 marks.

Activity

Read the analysis above.

- Identify where and how the student has used the sources evaluated in section C.
- Highlight sentences or phrases which show that the student is **analysing** the evidence from section B (that is, drawing conclusions and making judgments from the evidence rather than just stating the evidence).

Section E: Conclusion

This section is worth 2 marks. To get these marks you need to:

- **answer** the question that you set in your title
- make sure that your answer is based on the weight of evidence that you have presented.

Examiner's hints

As with section D, no new evidence should be introduced in this section.

You should write about 150–200 words in this section and you can err towards the lower end of the suggested word count.

> **Example section E: Conclusion**
>
> It is clear that conditions in the mining industry and discontent among miners played a key role in the build-up to the General Strike. These problems were intensified by broader economic issues in Britain and post-war Europe, leading to the decline of the economic situation nationally. Equally as important were the political issues, specifically the conflict between the left-wing trade unions and the right-wing government, and the potential association with the revolutionary Communist Party of Great Britain. Based on the weight of evidence, it was these political tensions, specifically in the months prior to the outbreak of the strike, that explain why a *general* strike happened in May 1926.

Section F: Referencing

This section is worth 3 marks. To get these 3 marks you need to:

- include accurate and consistent referencing **throughout** your IA
- reference all sources, written or otherwise, and include them in your list of sources at the end (note that references are required in sections B and D, but might also be necessary in sections C, A and E)
- provide a list of sources under section F which includes all citations (see below)
- use an appendix to attach any illustrations, documents, transcripts of interviews or other supporting evidence
- state the word count clearly and accurately on the title page – if the word count is not stated on the title page a maximum of 1 point is awarded.

Referencing systems

In essays you are expected to acknowledge the sources you use. You may not have to do this for every class essay you write, but both the IA and the extended essay require you to state clearly when you are using the work of other writers. This process is called citation. Each citation requires a reference at the end of your essay which gives full details of the source used.

If you do not do this, you can be accused of **plagiarism**.

Why is it necessary to include references?

It is necessary to acknowledge the sources that you are using for several reasons, namely:

- to provide evidence to your teacher and examiner of your wide reading
- to give credit to the original writer of the information you are using
- to allow the reader to follow up any quotes you give or any assertions you make by following your citation
- because it is good academic practice and you will be expected to use referencing in all essays and other written papers if you go on to further education.

How do you refer to works of authors in your essay?

Footnotes

One system (shown in the examples on pages 83–85 and 87–89) is to footnote any source that you have used at the bottom of your page of writing. Using superscript, you insert a number above the relevant place in the text (usually at the end of a sentence or quote) which links to the number of the footnote at the bottom of the page. Numbers are used consecutively throughout the essay. Your word processing program, for example Microsoft Word, will allow you do this very easily.

You should insert a footnote every time you quote directly from a source or use specific information from it, for example statistics.

Sometimes you can also use footnotes to add a brief extra piece of information that would be inappropriate in the main body of the text, perhaps to explain who a person was or the meaning of a word.

When giving the footnote, you should give the full details of the source you have used the first time you refer to it, along with the page number the information appears on. One way of doing this is shown below. There are several variations to this, for example the date is often given in parentheses and may appear after the publisher.

The reference lists:

- author
- date of publication
- if the source is a book, its title in italics; if the source is a newspaper or journal article or a report, its title in inverted commas
- details of publication (town or city it was published in, followed by publisher)
- volume and issue number (if necessary)
- page numbers (preceded by an abbreviation for 'page': 'pg.' or 'p.').

Use commas to separate each item of the citation and end with a full stop.

For example:

Barrass, G., 2009, *The Great Cold War: A Journey Through the Hall of Mirrors,* Stanford CA: Stanford University Press, pg. 88.

If your next footnote comes from the same source, you can use the Latin abbreviation *ibid.*, which is short for *ibidem*, meaning 'the same place', with the page number.

If the same text is used some time later, you can avoid writing out the full details of the source again by giving only the author's name then using the Latin abbreviation *op. cit.*, an abbreviation of the Latin phrase *opus citatum est,* meaning 'the work has been cited', and the page number.

See below for an example of how this works.

1 Barrass, G., 2009, *The Great Cold War: A Journey Through the Hall of Mirrors,* Stanford CA: Stanford University Press, p. 88.
2 Barrass, G., *ibid.*, p. 90.
3 Short, A., 2009, *The Origins of The Vietnam War,* New York: Longman, p. 79.
4 Barrass, G., *op. cit.*, p. 99.

Alternatively, you can use the 'short form' instead of *op. cit.*, which involves giving the author's name and title of book only for all citations from that book after the first one:

1 Barrass, G., 2009, *The Great Cold War: A Journey Through the Hall of Mirrors,* Stanford, CA: Stanford University Press, p. 88.
2 Short, A., 1989, *The Origins of The Vietnam War,* New York: Longman, p. 79.
3 Barrass, G., *The Great Cold War: A Journey Through the Hall of Mirrors,* p. 99.

Examiner's hints

It is vital that you are consistent in the referencing system you use. For example, if you are using *ibid.* and *op. cit.*, make sure you consistently use this system throughout your essay.

Also be consistent with your punctuation, font and formatting.

If all the references are put at the end of a text rather than at the end of each page, they are known as endnotes.

Guidelines on citing different sources

How do I reference:

- information from an author that is used in another text (i.e. a second-hand reference)?
  Bornet, V. D. as cited in Vivienne Saunders, *The USA and Vietnam 1945–75*, 2007, London: Hodder Murray, p. 99.

- an article?
  Ruane, K., 'The US in Asia: Vietnam', *Modern History Review*, Volume 14, No. 4, April 2003, pp. 13–16.

- a book that has more than one author?
  Gelb, L. and Betts, R., 1979, *The Irony of Vietnam*, Washington: Brookings Institution Press, pg. 6.

- a book that includes essays by different authors?
  Major Problems in the History of the Vietnam War, ed. Robert J. McMahon, 1990, Lexington DC: Heath and Company, pg. 127.

- information from a website?
  Try to give as much information as possible. Include the exact URL of the web page and the date that you visited it, for example:

  letter from Eisenhower to Diem, 1954,
  www.pbs.org/wgbh/amex/vietnam/psources/index.html
  Accessed 14 May 2011.

  Or, for an article:

  Prados, J., 'Vietnam: The history of an unwinnable war, 1945-1975', 2009,
  www.wilsoncenter.org/ondemand/index.cfm?fuseaction=home.
  play&mediaid=17E5D9F7-D8D4-8A24-2DE7F46F24935797
  Accessed 14 May 2011.

The Harvard System of referencing

Another way of indicating the sources that you have used is through the Harvard System. In this system, the author and the date of publication are included within the actual text itself – at the relevant point, in parentheses. If you are referring to a specific quote or part of the text, then the page reference goes in as well.

- When making reference to an author's work in your text, his or her name is followed by the year of publication of the work:
  It now seems clear that Stalin played a key role in the origins of the Cold War (Gaddis, 1997).
  Or, for a direct quote:
  Gaddis (1997, pg. 292) states that '… as long as Stalin was running the Soviet Union a cold war was unavoidable'.

- For a second-hand source:
  Sowcroft (cited in Barrass, 2009) states that it was remarkable that the West prevailed in the Cold War.

- For a website, state the authorship of the website and the date of the publication you are using.

- As with the footnote system, the full details of each reference is then put at the end in your bibliography or reference list. This list of sources is arranged alphabetically by author's name.

List of references or bibliography

This should be included at the end of your essay. Again, it is vital that you are rigorous and consistent in your style and formatting.

Your reference for each source used for a book must include:

author's surname, initials, year of the book's publication, title of the book, place of publication (this must be a town or city, not a country), publisher.

If the source is an article in a journal, you must include the article's title, name of the journal and volume and issue numbers (if appropriate).

If you have inserted footnotes, this is the same information that you will have put in your first footnote referring to a source. However, the key thing is that all references here are in **alphabetical order by author's name.**

For example:

Barrass, G., 2009, *The Great Cold War: A Journey Through the Hall of Mirrors,* Stanford CA: Stanford University Press.

McMahon, R. J., (ed.), 1990, *Major Problems in the History of the Vietnam War,* Lexington DC: Heath and Company.

(See the section on footnotes for how to reference other kinds of text, including websites.)

Example historical investigation

This is an example of a complete IA with examiner's comments.

History HL Internal Assessment

Name:

School:

Candidate number:

Word count: 1,997

> To what extent did Germany sign the Treaty of Rapallo in April 1922 because of fears of an expansionist Poland?

Examiner's hints

Another standardized method that is commonly used for footnotes and endnotes is the Chicago method. See http://owl.english.purdue.edu/owl/resource/717/01/

A useful website to help you to collate and then create a thorough and accurate list of sources is noodletools: www.noodletools.com

Another useful website which will also allow you to collate your sources and show you how to format them is: www.citethisforme.com.

Examiner's comment

The research question is clearly stated. Method and scope are developed and closely focused on research question.

3 marks

Section A: Plan of the investigation

The following question will be investigated: To what extent did Germany sign the Treaty of Rapallo in April 1922 because of fears of an expansionist Poland? First, cross-reference evidence from a range of sources, including the analysis of historians, will be gathered. An analysis of the role played by the fear of Poland will be included, but also the economic and military reasons for Germany signing Rapallo will be analysed. The scope of the research is primarily the years 1918–22. The sources used will be evaluated, with particular focus on two sources that are significant as they provide key evidence for two opposing lines of argument – Michael Laffan's *The Burden of German History 1919–1945: Essays for the Goethe Institute* and the text of the Treaty of Rapallo (Avalon Project – Documents in Law, History and Diplomacy, Yale University). A conclusion will then be reached based on the weight of the evidence and evaluation of the sources.

Section B: A summary of evidence

Fears of an expansionist Poland

'Co-operation against Poland', was a 'traditional German Russian' policy move.[1]

In the Three Partitions of Poland in the 18th century the Prussians and Russians had carved the state up to restore the balance of power in the East.[2]

Along with Anti-Polish Reforms during early Imperial Germany, there were plans in 1916 for the German military to take Poland and resettle it with Germans.[3]

Poland had shown itself to be expansionist in the 1919–1921 Polish-Soviet War and Jozef Pilsduski noted: 'All that we can gain in the west depends on the Entente – on the extent to which it may wish to squeeze Germany', while in the east 'there are doors that open and close, and it depends on who forces them open and how far'.[4]

The 1921 Treaty of Riga signed between Poland and France made Germany fear encirclement.[5]

Plebiscite over Silesia in 1921 inflamed opinion against Poland in Germany.[6]

'Germany was even vulnerable to invasion by a second-rank power such as Poland whose army was twice the size of the Reichswehr.'[7]

Economic reasons

'German demand for new markets was mirrored by the desperate need of the weakened Soviet state for foreign aid and capital investment.'[8]

1920 increased unofficial economic contacts between Germans and Russians.[9]

6 May 1921: German and Soviet provisional commercial agreements were signed and Lenin introduced NEP reforms allowing limited private enterprise.[10]

Russia rescinded claims of war damages against Germany (Article 116 of the Versailles Treaty entitled Russia to possible war damages) and promised most-favoured nation status to each other.[11]

1 Hiden, J. W., 1986, *The Weimar Republic (Seminar Studies in History)*, London: Longman Publishing Group, pg. 26.

2 Bideleux, R. and Jeffries, I., 1998, *A History of Eastern Europe: Crisis and change*, London: Routledge, pg. 156.

3 Giles, G., Pape, W. and Bullivant, K., 1999, *Germany and Eastern Europe: Cultural identities and cultural differences (Yearbook of European Studies/Annuaire d'études Européennes*, 13). London: European Cultural Foundation/Fondation Européenne de Culture, pg. 28.

4 MacMillan, M., 2003, *Paris 1919: Six months that changed the world*, New York: Random House Trade Paperbacks.

5 Hiden, J. W., *op. cit.*, pg. 26.

6 Hiden, J. W., *op. cit.*, pg. 27.

7 Laffan, M., 1989, *The Burden of German History 1919–45: Essays for the Goethe Institute*, Dublin: Methuen Publishing Ltd, pg. 83.

8 Hiden, J. W., *op. cit.*, pg. 26.

9 Hiden, J. W., *op. cit.* pg. 27.

10 Hiden, J. W., *op. cit.* pg. 27.

11 Hiden, J. W., *op. cit.* pg. 28.

Article 5: 'Both governments shall regard the industrial needs of their countries in a mutually favourable spirit.'[12]

'In May 1921, the governments revoked the law that had nationalised all branches of industry.'[13] NEP Policy of Lenin.

'A Russian peace treaty left open the possibility of the Soviets paying off Czarist debts to the West in exchange for the right to collect reparations from Germany – under Article 116 of the Versailles Treaty. In January 1922 Karl Radek... told (the Germans) that the French had made such an offer to the Soviets.'[14]

Military reasons

Allows 'Germany's future secret development of military weapons' – unknown to political leaders' secret agreement.

In January 1920, Karl Radek, Lenin's agent in Berlin, met with German leaders about possible military collaboration.[15]

'refinement of Ministry of Defence after 1920' in Germany.[16]

Treaty of Rapallo would 'create in Russia an armaments industry which in case of need will serve us' economic leaders argue.[17]

'Von Stupganel and von Seeckt were more impatient to evade the disarmament clause and to revise Germany's boundaries in the East.'[18]

'The Reichswehr was determined to exploit to the full any opportunity to revise or undermine the Treaty of Versailles.'[19]

'regain her status as a great power' through agreements with other powers.[20]

'Only when the various limitations on her sovereignty had been removed could Germany expect to achieve her second major objective, territorial revision.'[21]

'It is also true that it prevented any revival of the old Triple Entente.'[22]

---

12 'The Avalon Project: German-Russian Agreement; April 16, 1922 (Treaty of Rapallo).' Avalon Project – Documents in Law, History and Diplomacy. Yale University, n.d. Accessed 5 January 2010. http://avalon.law.yale.edu/20th_century/rapallo_001.asp

13 Kenez, P., 2006, *A History of the Soviet Union from the Beginning to the End*, second edn., New York: Cambridge University Press, pg. 90.

14 Spaulding, K. M., *op. cit.*, pg. 184.

15 Hiden, J. W., *op. cit.*, pg. 26.

16 Hiden, J. W., *op. cit.*, pg. 54.

17 Lee, S. J., 1998, *The Weimar Republic (Questions and Analysis in History)*, New York: Routledge, pg. 83.

18 Lee, S., *op. cit.*, pg. 79.

19 Lee, S., *op. cit.*, pg. 83.

20 Laffan, M., *op. cit.*, pg. 84.

21 Laffan, M., *op. cit.*, pg. 86.

22 Taylor, A. J. P., 1991, *The Origins of the Second World War*, (Penguin History), London: Penguin Books Ltd, pg. 76.

Examiner's comment

Factual material is all relevant to the investigation. The material is well researched and organized. It is correctly referenced.

6 marks

Section C: An evaluation of sources

Laffan, M., 1989, *The Burden of German History 1919–45: Essays for the Goethe Institute,* Dublin: Methuen Publishing Ltd.

This source's origin is valuable as it was written by a prominent historian, Michael Laffan. Professor Laffan is a lecturer in both Irish and European history and has published many articles for academic journals, which gives him the value of experience and education. The fact that he was chosen to chair and edit a series of lectures about German history between 1919–1945 suggests he is considered a valuable source of knowledge by his peers.

This source is also valuable because its purpose is to analyse German history in the same scope as my essay question. It looks only at the Weimar Republic and Nazi Germany and would therefore look at short-term reasons for the treaty, making it valuable for my question.

However, the source's purpose is to give lectures for the Goethe Institute, which is funded by the German Foreign Office and Press Office, and this suggests political motivations behind the work. The lectures were given in 1988 when Germany was still divided and most lecturers focus on how the Weimar Republic was doomed to fail. This possible political purpose and the context limits the source.

Finally, as an Irish historian who focuses on Irish, German and European history, Laffan might be limited as a source of information. Unlike a writer well-versed in German history or who has concentrated solely on this area, Laffan has published no other books on German history, suggesting this is not his primary field of research and limiting the source.

**'The Avalon Project : German-Russian Agreement; April 16, 1922 (Treaty of Rapallo).' Avalon Project – Documents in Law, History and Diplomacy. Yale University, n.d. Accessed 5 January 2010.
http://avalon.law.yale.edu/20th_century/rapallo_001.asp**

The source was signed by the German foreign minister, Walther Rathenau, which makes it valuable as the German foreign minister was responsible for foreign affairs for the Weimar Republic. Therefore, it is an important source in analysing German foreign policy and German foreign motivations.

The source's purpose also makes it valuable for my question. The purpose was to bind the two governments to legal agreements and therefore it is a valuable source in determining what agreements the Germans were willing to legally bind to. This possibly makes the source valuable in looking for what reasons the Germans signed the treaty as some of their aims would be embedded in the treaty's stipulations in 1922.

However, the source is also limited because it is simply the treaty agreements. Rather than showing the negotiation or fully stating the reasons Germany signed the treaty in 1922, it shows what both sides were willing to agree to, making it limited in breadth for looking at German reasons for signing the treaty and therefore limited in its scope.

Finally, this treaty's purpose was only to make public what clauses the Germans and Russians agreed to. The secret clauses were not signed until later and this suggests that the source would be limited in understanding some of the German military reasons for signing the treaty.

Examiner's comment

There is evaluation of the sources and explicit reference to their origin, purpose, value and limitation.

5 marks

Section D: Analysis

The Treaty of Rapallo signed between the Soviet Union and Germany in 1922 has long been seen as the cooperation of the two pariah states of Europe and the first steps to German rearmament. The political and diplomatic isolation of Germany and Russia that ensued after their defeats in the First World War has been seen as drawing them together. German reasons for signing the treaty include long-term and short-term fears of Poland, economic reasons and military reasons.

Since the 18th century Germany and Russia had a mutual distrust of Poland which can be seen as a reason for the two signing Rapallo. At the three partitions of Poland[1] they had sought to balance out their zones of influence in Eastern Europe. 'Co-operations against Poland'[2] was traditional between the two powers and there were plans in 1916 to seize Poland and resettle it with Germans.[3] The creation of a Polish state by Versailles directly threatened the previous balance of power that Germany had attempted to establish and cooperation with Russia could lead to re-establishing this.

Furthermore, Polish actions after Versailles threatened German interests. The Polish Leader Pilsduski noted 'All that we can gain in the west depends on the Entente – on the extent to which it may wish to squeeze Germany'[4] and the Treaty of Riga signed between Poland and France in 1921 was threatening to Germany.[5] This, along with the plebiscite over Silesia in 1921 being ignored and given to Poland, 'inflamed opinion against Poland in Germany'.[6] These two actions threatened further German territorial losses, something that would endanger the Weimar Republic and be unacceptable for Germany. Therefore their aims at Rapallo were to establish an alliance against Poland.

Finally, militarily Versailles had enacted strict limitations for the Germans, meaning that the Polish military was twice the size of the Reichswehr.[7] The fear of an expansionist Poland with a larger military than Germany meant Germany sought an eastern ally, and therefore signed Rapallo for this purpose.

However, Germany had economic reasons for signing the treaty and my evaluation of the Treaty suggests there were many economic agreements made between the two. 'German demand for new markets were mirrored by the desperate need of the weakened state for foreign aid and capital investment' which suggests a mutual benefit from economic ties between the two nations.[8] Even by 1920 there were increased unofficial economic contacts between the Germans and the Russians.[9] The announcement of the NEP by Lenin[10] and the commercial deal on the 6 May 1921 were signs of the need for larger economic ties between the two nations. Therefore, the Treaty of Rapallo can be seen as the consolidation of these economic agreements, including provisions that gave each side

1 Bideleux R., and Jeffries, I., *op. cit.*, pg. 156.
2 Hiden, J. W., *op. cit.*, pg. 26.
3 Giles, G., Pape, W. and Bullivant, K., *op. cit.*, pg. 28.
4 MacMillan, M., *op. cit.*
5 Hiden, J. W., *op. cit.*, pg. 26.
6 Hiden, J. W., *op. cit.*, pg. 27.
7 Laffan, M., *op. cit.*, pg. 83.
8 Laffan, J., *op. cit.*, pg. 83.
9 Hiden, J. W., *op. cit.*, pg. 27.
10 Hiden, J. W., *op. cit.*, pg. 27.

a most favoured clause[11] and the Germans' freedom from nationalization of their investment.[12]

Another economic reason was clause 116 of the Versailles Treaty, which entitled the Russians to possible reparations from the Germans.[13] Karl Radek stated in January 1922 to the Germans that there was a possibility of renounced Czarist debt being paid back through reparations from Germany.[14] The contentious issue of reparation and the increased burden it would put on the German economy could be devastating. Therefore, Rapallo was a way to formalize relations and rescind wartime agreements, which would free Germany from this potential obligation and ensure the Allies could not pressure the Soviets.

However, there were also military reasons for signing the treaty as the restrictions of Versailles meant the Germans could not develop modern weapons such as submarines, airplanes and tanks. The vast lands of Russia would allow 'Germany's future secret development of military weapons'.[15] Meetings with Karl Radek in January 1920 suggested possible military collaboration[16] and this met well with Germany's goal of 'refinement of the ministry of defence after 1920'.[17] The agreement would 'create in Russia an armaments industry which in case of need will serve us', German leaders argued.[18]

These military reasons also fell in line with military leaders' points of view. 'Von Stupganel and von Seeckt were impatient to evade the disarmament clause'[19] and felt 'only when various limitations on her sovereignty had been removed could Germany expect to achieve her second major objective, territorial revision'.[20] Signing the first formal treaty with Soviet Russia not only had military benefits but also could be part of the German military's long-term goal of territorial revision. However, my evaluation of Laffan's lecture suggests that military reasons may have been over-emphasized because of the post-war context.

11 Hiden, J. W., *op. cit.*, pg. 28.
12 Translation of the Treaty of Rapallo by the Secretariat of the League of Nations, *League of Nations Treaty Series*, Volume 19 327L 1923, pg. 250 et seq. and Translation of the Supplementary Agreement to the German-Russian Agreement, concluded at Rapallo, April 16, 1922, signed at Berlin, November 5, 1922, Volume 26 327L 1924, pg. 391 et seq.
13 Spaulding, R. M., 1997, *Osthandel and Ostpolitik: German foreign trade policies in Eastern Europe from Bismarck to Adenauer* (Monographs in German History, Vol 1), Oxford: Berghahn Books, pg. 184.
14 Spaulding, R. M., *op. cit.*, pg. 184.
15 Hiden, J. W., *op. cit.*, pg. 26.
16 Hiden, J. W., *op. cit.*, pg. 26.
17 Hiden, J. W., *op. cit.*, pg. 58.
18 Lee, S., *op. cit.*, pg. 83.
19 Lee, S., *op. cit.*, pg. 79.
20 Laffan, J., *op. cit.*, pg. 86.

Examiner's comment

There is critical analysis of the evidence presented in section B, accurate referencing and an awareness of the significance to the investigation of the sources evaluated in section C. Different interpretations are analysed.

6 marks

Section E: Conclusion

Military reasons seem to have been over-emphasized after Hitler's rearmament programme and the unveiling of German planes in 1933, but it does not disregard the fact that most political leaders did not know about the military provisions. This suggests that the need to prevent Polish expansionism was the primary reason for Germany signing the treaty of Rapallo. The implications of a strong Poland backed by a strong French ally were similar to the encirclement created pre-1914. Economic reasons were mutually beneficial and seem to be more a by-product of diplomatic ties and agreements than would have happened through other relationships, suggested by the increased economic contacts in 1920. It would therefore seem that in 1922 it was the 'Polish problem' that allowed the two pariah states to overcome their ideological differences and sign the treaty of Rapallo.

Total word count: 1,997

Examiner's comment

The conclusion is clearly stated and consistent with the evidence presented.

2 marks

Section F: List of sources

Website

'The Avalon Project : German-Russian Agreement; April 16, 1922 (Treaty of Rapallo).' Avalon Project – Documents in Law, History and Diplomacy. Yale University, n.d. Accessed 5 January 2010. http://avalon.law.yale.edu/20th_century/rapallo_001.asp

Books

Bideleux R. and Jeffries, I., 1998, *A History of Eastern Europe: Crisis and change,* London: Routledge.

Giles, G., Pape, W. and Bullivant, K., 1999, *Germany and Eastern Europe: Cultural identities and cultural differences* (Yearbook of European Studies/Annuaire d'études Européennes, 13). London: European Cultural Foundation/Fondation Européene de Culture.

Hiden, J. W., 1986, *The Weimar Republic (Seminar Studies in History),* London: Longman.

Kenez, P., 2006, *A History of the Soviet Union from the Beginning to the End,* second edn., New York: Cambridge University Press.

Laffan, M., 1989, *The Burden of German History 1919–45: Essays for the Goethe Institute.* Dublin: Methuen Publishing Ltd.

Lee, S. J., 1998, *The Weimar Republic (Questions and Analysis in History),* New York: Routledge.

MacMillan, M., 2003, *Paris 1919: Six months that changed the world,* New York: Random House.

Rohl, J. C. G., 1970, *From Bismarck to Hitler: The problem of continuity in German history,* (Problems and Perspectives in History), New York: Longman.

Spaulding, R. M., 1997, *Osthandel and Ostpolitik: German foreign trade policies in Eastern Europe from Bismarck to Adenauer* (Monographs in German History, Vol 1), Oxford: Berghahn Books.

Taylor, A. J. P., 1991, *The Origins of the Second World War,* (Penguin History), London: Penguin Books Ltd.

Examiner's comment

An appropriate list of sources, using one standard method, is included.

The investigation is within the word limit.

3 marks

Activity

Before handing in your IA, complete this checklist.

Check that you have:	✓
included your research question in the plan of the investigation	
fully referenced all sources used in both the evidence and analysis sections	
used your two sources from section C as part of your evidence in section B and analysis in section D	
included a contents page	
cited all sources at the end, using a standard system	
used a range of relevant sources – including those of key historians writing on your topic	
kept within the 2,000 word limit and put your word count clearly on your cover page	
included supporting documents and illustrations in an appendix	

Not all of you will be doing an extended essay in history. However, if you enjoy the subject, then this is an opportunity to apply yourself in an in-depth extended research task and to become an expert on a specific historical topic. If you are considering choosing to study history at college or university level, then you should definitely choose this as your extended essay subject, as you can cite your question on your university applications or personal statements. Working on your extended essay will have given you first-hand experience of historical research and you will be able to discuss your work at any interviews you have during your application process. It is an element of the diploma course that sets you apart from students taking other courses as it is a rigorously academic piece of work.

What is the extended essay?

It is a piece of personal research into a topic of your choice which has to be presented in the format of a formal research paper of around 4,000 words.

How do I choose a topic?

This is completely up to you and it does not have to be part of the IB Diploma Programme that you have studied. However, there are some key considerations which you need to bear in mind when choosing the topic:

- It should be a 'narrow' topic which allows you to analyse effectively within 4,000 words. For example, if your interest is the Second World War, limit yourself to investigating the role of one person; a particular battle; or a limited geographical area, such as a village, town or region.
- Find a topic that will allow you to investigate a historical question and to carry out analysis rather than a description (see pages 65–66).
- You should not choose a topic from the last 10 years as there will not yet be enough objective written resources to make this a worthwhile investigation.
- Consider what resources are available to you. If you are writing your extended essay over the summer vacation, for example, consider where you will be and if this will give you access to any useful sources. Check that the books you want to use are in the library or can be ordered easily.

Do not plan to use only Internet sites (see page 104). If you plan to use local sources, for example from local archives, check that these are accessible to you.

- Your chosen topic must clearly be a history topic – if it overlaps with art, psychology or economics it must still be dealt with as a historical investigation from a historical perspective.
- You should be genuinely interested in the topic you choose.

'Research questions that do not lead to systematic investigation, critical analysis and detailed understanding are unlikely to be suitable.'
IB DIPLOMA PROGRAMME EXTENDED ESSAY GUIDE, MARCH 2007, PG. 81

How do I choose a research question?

Once you have a topic, you need to decide what question you can ask within that topic. This will involve reading around your topic to find out what the key issues are and where there could be an opportunity for historical debate and analysis. This could involve:

- skim reading specialized history books to identify key issues (see page 8)
- searching for articles on your topic which cover certain angles and/or raise controversial questions
- consulting your school or college librarian to help you find whether there has been any other research in this area; the librarian may be able to find other research papers on your topic for you and you can then read the abstracts to these papers.

It is unlikely that you will start off with your perfect question. You will probably start with a few possible questions and will need to discuss and refine these with your supervisor in order to get to your final question. For example, a student who chooses the Rwandan genocide as a topic might initially want to focus on the legacy of imperialism but find that there is more evidence on the role of international community at the time, including the UN, and so would switch the focus.

Here are some examples of topics and questions used for extended essays that have led to effective investigations.

Topic	Non-intervention in the Spanish Civil War
Question	Why did Britain pursue a policy of non-intervention in the Spanish Civil War during 1936?
Topic	The Mau Mau Rebellion
Question	To what extent were British economic policies towards the Kikuyu tribe the main cause of the Mau Mau rebellion of 1952 in Kenya?
Topic	The Malayan Emergency
Question	To what extent was the British victory against the communists during the Malayan Emergency due mainly to the actions of the High Commissioner, General Templer?
Topic	The Danish Resistance Movement in the Second World War
Question	To what extent was the Danish Resistance Movement successful in disrupting the Nazi occupation of Denmark (1940–1945)?
Topic	The Second World War in Asia
Question	To what extent was the Jaywick Raid on Singapore Harbour in 1943 successful?
Topic	The 'troubles' in Northern Ireland
Question	To what extent was the Battle of the Bogside in August 1969 in Northern Ireland brought about by the actions of civil rights activists?

Topic	The RAF's policy regarding bombing of Auschwitz
Question	To what extent was the RAF'S decision not to bomb the Auschwitz Concentration Camp, between 1941 and 1944, based on military reasons?
Topic	The Falklands/Malvinas War 1982
Question	How significant was the role of Galtieri in determining the outcome of the Malvinas War?
Topic	The Nigerian Civil War, 1967–1970
Question	How significant was the role of foreign mercenaries in the Biafran army?

Your supervisor

At all stages in the process of writing your extended essay, you will have the opportunity to work closely with your supervisor. Your supervisor will discuss with you your choice of topic and question, will guide you in your research and in your writing of the essay – checking (though not editing) your draft essay. When you have handed in your essay, your supervisor will also interview you about it. In all, your supervisor will probably spend around 3–5 hours helping you and it is a good idea to keep on good terms with your supervisor, for example by sticking to deadlines!

The research process

Finding sources

Start looking for sources as soon as you have identified the topic you are interested in. You will ultimately need around 20 different sources. These should include a range of both primary and secondary sources, books and articles by historians and relevant websites. Note that you should have a mix of these sources and overreliance on one type of source, for example Internet sources, could penalize you in criteria C of the mark scheme.

Talk to your supervisor and your librarian about useful books and articles (see the list on the next page). You also need to be critical in your use of sources and keep in mind the source evaluation skills that you have developed for Paper 1 and also your IA. You will be expected at some point in your extended essay to comment on the value and limitations of the sources that you have used (see pages 39–40).

> **Where can you find useful resources?**
>
> - Your library may have access to Questia (or another online library); you can access thousands of books and periodicals through this library.
> - Check bookshops online (such as Amazon) to see what books have been published on the topic that you plan to study. Check dates of publication (to ensure they include up-to-date research) and reviews.
> - Find websites with useful articles such as Google Scholar. Always check the credentials of any author whose work you read online.
> - If you have a university or further education nearby, check to see if you can use its library.
> - Investigate museums on your topic; often these have archives.
> - Don't forget memoirs, biographies and autobiographies by key figures.
> - For primary sources also consider diaries, government papers and public broadcasts.
> - Can you interview anyone about your topic? If so, the interview will need to be written up and included in an appendix.
> - Look at the references of any article or book that you read as this may lead you to other useful sources.

Reading and note taking

Make sure that you make a note of all sources you use along with the page numbers of all specific information and quotes. This will be essential for your footnotes (or endnotes) and the referencing section at the end of your essay.

Follow the guidelines set out on pages 8–9 on how to read effectively. Use the note-taking techniques outlined on pages 9–16 to record all your findings.

Writing the essay

Structure

You should follow the following structure in writing your essay:

- title page
- abstract
- contents page
- introduction
- body of the essay – it is advisable to divide this into chapters which will help you structure and develop your argument
- conclusion
- references and bibliography
- appendices.

This is not the order in which you will write the essay, however.

It is probably best to start with the main body of the essay and once that is complete, come back to the introduction. The last parts that you write will be the conclusion, abstract, title page and contents page.

Using the assessment criteria

Your essay will be marked against a clear set of criteria which you should read carefully **before** writing your essay and which you should refer to regularly **during** the writing process. These criteria and marks are used for all IB Diploma Programme subjects. They are given below along with an introductory explanation of how they apply to an essay in history.

Extended essay assessment criteria

Criterion A: Research question

For your history essay, this means your question must be concerned with a meaningful historical question, it must be clearly worded and focused and it must be stated both in the abstract and in your introduction.

0 The research question is not stated in the introduction or does not lend itself to a systematic investigation in an extended essay in the subject in which it is registered.

1 The research question is stated in the introduction but is not clearly expressed or is too broad in scope to be treated effectively within the word limit.

2 The research question is clearly stated in the introduction and sharply focused, making effective treatment possible within the word limit.

Criterion B: Introduction

Do not use this as an opportunity to give lots of descriptive background to your topic! Instead, you should use the introduction to explain why your topic is worth researching and to put it into context.

0 Little or no attempt is made to set the research question into context. There is little or no attempt to explain the significance of the topic.

1 Some attempt is made to set the research question into context. There is some attempt to explain the significance of the topic and why it is worthy of investigation.

2 The context of the research question is clearly demonstrated. The introduction clearly explains the significance of the topic and why it is worthy of investigation.

Criterion C: Investigation

This criterion assesses your collection and use of sources. As explained on page 104, you need to use a variety of primary and secondary sources in your essay and to use historiography where appropriate to support your arguments.

0 There is little or no evidence that sources have been consulted or data gathered, and little or no evidence of planning in the investigation.

1 A range of inappropriate sources has been consulted, or inappropriate data has been gathered, and there is little evidence that the investigation has been planned.

2 A limited range of appropriate sources has been consulted, or data has been gathered, and some relevant material has been selected. There is evidence of some planning in the investigation.

3 A sufficient range of appropriate sources has been consulted, or data has been gathered, and relevant material has been selected. The investigation has been satisfactorily planned.

4 An imaginative range of appropriate sources has been consulted, or data has been gathered, and relevant material has been carefully selected. The investigation has been well planned.

Criterion D: Knowledge and understanding of the topic studied

This criterion is testing your in-depth knowledge – your essay should indicate that you have a genuine understanding of the issues that you cover, including any historical debate.

0 The essay demonstrates no real knowledge or understanding of the topic studied.

1 The essay demonstrates some knowledge but little understanding of the topic studied. The essay shows little awareness of an academic context for the investigation.

2 The essay demonstrates an adequate knowledge and some understanding of the topic studied. The essay shows some awareness of an academic context for the investigation.

3 The essay demonstrates a good knowledge and understanding of the topic studied. Where appropriate, the essay successfully outlines an academic context for the investigation.

4 The essay demonstrates a very good knowledge and understanding of the topic studied. Where appropriate, the essay clearly and precisely locates the investigation in an academic context.

Criterion E: Reasoned argument

This is where the essay-writing skills that you have been developing for Papers 2 and 3 come in to good use. You need to ensure that you have structured your answer so that it clearly develops an argument which addresses the question that you have set. Refer back to pages 65–66 for suggestions on how to structure your essay in an analytical way. All your arguments also need to be supported with precise evidence.

0 There is no attempt to develop a reasoned argument in relation to the research question.

1 There is a limited or superficial attempt to present ideas in a logical and coherent manner, and to develop a reasoned argument in relation to the research question.

2 There is some attempt to present ideas in a logical and coherent manner, and to develop a reasoned argument in relation to the research question, but this is only partially successful.

3 Ideas are presented in a logical and coherent manner, and a reasoned argument is developed in relation to the research question, but with some weaknesses.

4 Ideas are presented clearly and in a logical and coherent manner. The essay succeeds in developing a reasoned and convincing argument in relation to the research question.

Criterion F: Application of analytical and evaluative skills appropriate to the subject

As already stated, you need to ensure that you remain analytical rather than descriptive in your approach to answering the question. You also need to use your analytical skills to comment on the evidence that you have used. As with the IA, you need to be aware of the value and limitations of the sources that you are using. However, unlike in the IA, you should not have a separate section in your essay addressing this. Rather, you should incorporate comments on the sources that you have used into the main body of the essay.

0 The essay shows no application of appropriate analytical and evaluative skills.

1 The essay shows little application of appropriate analytical and evaluative skills.

2 The essay shows some application of appropriate analytical and evaluative skills, which may be only partially effective.

3 The essay shows sound application of appropriate analytical and evaluative skills.

4 The essay shows effective and sophisticated application of appropriate analytical and evaluative skills.

Criterion G: Use of language appropriate to the subject

As with any good essay writing in history, you need to ensure that you use the historical terminology appropriate to your topic. Also avoid generalizations, vague unsupported assertions or colloquial language.

0   The language used is inaccurate and unclear. There is no effective use of terminology appropriate to the subject.

1   The language used sometimes communicates clearly but does not do so consistently. The use of terminology appropriate to the subject is only partly accurate.

2   The language used for the most part communicates clearly. The use of terminology appropriate to the subject is usually accurate.

3   The language used communicates clearly. The use of terminology appropriate to the subject is accurate, although there may be occasional lapses.

4   The language used communicates clearly and precisely. Terminology appropriate to the subject is used accurately, with skill and understanding.

Criterion H: Conclusion

Your conclusion should answer your question. It should also reflect the weight of your arguments and evidence in the main body of your essay; there should be no surprises and no new evidence presented in your conclusion.

0   Little or no attempt is made to provide a conclusion that is relevant to the research question.

1   A conclusion is attempted that is relevant to the research question but may not be entirely consistent with the evidence presented in the essay.

2   An effective conclusion is clearly stated; it is relevant to the research question and consistent with the evidence presented in the essay. It should include unresolved questions where appropriate to the subject concerned.

Criterion I: Formal presentation

It should be easy to get full marks in this section. You need to ensure that you include in your essay all of the following required elements: title page, table of contents, page numbers. You also need to ensure that you follow the guidelines for referencing and bibliography set out on pages 90–93. Keeping to the word count of 4,000 words is also essential. You can include an appendix with information that you think is relevant, such as maps or tables of statistics, but this must be mentioned in the essay via footnotes to make it worthwhile including.

0   The formal presentation is unacceptable, or the essay exceeds 4,000 words.
1   The formal presentation is poor.
2   The formal presentation is satisfactory.
3   The formal presentation is good.
4   The formal presentation is excellent.

Criterion J: Abstract

This will probably be the last part of the essay that you write as it sets out your research question, the full scope of your essay and it also presents your conclusion. By reading an abstract the reader should have a clear idea of the contents of the extended essay.

0   The abstract exceeds 300 words or one or more of the required elements of an abstract is missing.

1   The abstract contains the elements listed above but they are not all clearly stated.

2   The abstract clearly states all the elements listed above.

Criterion K: Holistic judgment

Marks under this criterion are given to reward 'intellectual initiative'; that is, choosing a less well-explored topic or investigating an original angle on a topic and/or for 'insight and depth of understanding'.

0 The essay shows no evidence of such qualities.
1 The essay shows little evidence of such qualities.
2 The essay shows some evidence of such qualities.
3 The essay shows clear evidence of such qualities.
4 The essay shows considerable evidence of such qualities.

from *IB History guide* © International Baccalaureate 2008

Activity

Task 1

The abstract will probably be one of the last things you do. It is also something that you will have no experience of doing. Read the abstract below and check that it meets the requirements for criterion J. Highlight where it sets out:

- the research question
- the scope of the essay
- the conclusion of the essay.

To what extent was Juan Peron's fall from power in 1955 a consequence of Eva Peron's death?

Abstract

The objective of this essay is to assess the extent to which Juan Domingo Peron's fall from power in 1955 was a consequence of the death of Eva Peron.

This essay will firstly address issues contributing to Peron's downfall associated with Eva's death, for example the loss of popularity that arose from it. Other factors such as Eva's contribution to Argentinean politics and the depression into which Peron fell after her death will also be discussed.

However, it is not sufficient only to consider Eva's role in Peron's downfall; the wider context of life in Argentina is therefore reviewed. This essay will examine the economic pressures in Argentina in the 1940s and 1950s, focusing on the railway problems and the unemployment and strikes in the cities, highlighting the fact that Peron's political reforms and policies played a role in his downfall.

This essay will also consider the part played by Peron's disagreements with the church. It will address the issues arising from the successful competition with UES and the reasons why the short-term disagreements with the church were to blame for Peron's fall.

Finally, the military played an important role in Peron's fall from power and this essay will examine the reasons why this was so, for example the coups and strikes that finally determined Peron's fall.

Undoubtedly the death of Eva Peron contributed greatly to her husband's fall from power, both directly and indirectly. However, her death alone cannot explain the ending of Peron's regime. The conclusion of this essay is that it was the coincidence of all previously mentioned factors that brought about the end of Peron. Had any one factor been absent, his government may have survived.

Task 2

Read the introduction below.

Refer back to criterion B for getting full marks for an introduction. Highlight where the student has:

- explained why the topic is worthy of investigation
- put the topic into context.

> **To what extent was the Battle of the Bogside in August 1969 in Northern Ireland brought about by the actions of the civil rights activists?**
>
> **Introduction**
>
> In August 1979, the 'troubles' in Northern Ireland were drastically brought to the attention of the British public, and were catapulted to the forefront of British politics for nearly 30 years. This topic is very significant as the 'troubles' in Northern Ireland continued up until the good Friday Agreement in 1998, with the conflict often spilling over to the British mainland as the IRA bombed targets in London, Brighton and several other cities in the United Kingdom.
>
> The Battle of the Bogside began in Derry, where the Protestant Apprentice Boys' Parade turned into a standoff between the Catholic dominated Bogside area and the local police, the Royal Ulster Constabulary, ending in several violent clashes between 12 and 14 August. These riots were echoed across Northern Ireland, including in the capital, Belfast, with many smaller riots breaking out across the country. There are many reasons why the rioting and clashes with the police began, such as a long history of religious division in the country and the actions of the British government. However, one of the main triggers was the development of a civil rights movement in Northern Ireland.

Task 3

The extract below is **one** chapter from the main body of the extended essay: **Why did Britain pursue a policy of non-intervention in the Spanish Civil War during 1936?**

Refer back to the extended essay criteria on pages 105-108 and consider how far this extract meets the requirement of the criteria set out in D (knowledge and understanding of the topic studied), E (reasoned argument), F (application of analytical and evaluative skills appropriate to the subject) and G (use of language appropriate to the subject).

> **The goal of non-intervention was to prevent Italian or German expansion**
>
> Rather than merely appeasing the aggressors to prevent the spread of war from Spain, Britain can also be seen as astutely using diplomacy to limit intervention in Spain, thus limiting any upset of the balance of the Mediterranean. The British can be seen as creating a policy of non-intervention, and subsequently the Non-Intervention Committee, to prevent German or Italian aid from escalating to levels with which those countries would be able to gain concessions from Franco. The existence of the committee meant that aid would be limited and partially clandestine. This committee relied on Britain constantly pursuing strict non-intervention.
>
> As stated in Secret British Foreign Office Documents, Britain was concerned with the possibility that the Spanish Civil War would lead to 'Italy taking some action which might upset the existing balance in the Western Mediterranean'.[1] Key to British trade were the Straits of Gibraltar and the Suez Canal which 'in a war with a European Power would be essential to (British interests).'[2] The ultimate fear was that because Italy had little control in the Mediterranean it would attempt to aid Spain in the hope of gaining more power which would 'make (British) control of the Straits and use of Gibraltar as a naval and air base extremely difficult'.[3] Explicitly it is not an ideological argument as the documents state, 'whether Fascist or Communist emerge from the present struggle the question of the security of our base at Gibraltar will require serious examination'.[4] Further suggesting
>
> ---
>
> 1 Cabinet Office Paper 'Western Med: Situation arising from the Spanish Civil War', Eden. A., Foreign Office, London. 31 August 1936. Accessed 5 September 2009.
> 2 *ibid.*
> 3 *ibid.*
> 4 *ibid.*

it is Italy that Britain was concerned with, the document states 'Italy is the only enemy, in contemplation'.[5]

All this information led to statements concluding that a policy of non-intervention would be pursued, as 'if a universal agreement can be reached and enforced there would be no reason for the winning side in Spain to grant territorial concessions'. Therefore British policy was directed against Italy and non-intervention was a way of limiting Italian aid so Italy could gain no concessions in the Mediterranean that would interfere with British power.

At the beginning of the crisis Britain saw the need to prevent the Axis from intervening at all, but as the crisis played out the British had to prevent large-scale German and Italian aid entering which could turn the tide of war and grant the Axis concessions in the Mediterranean. By early August 1936, Germany and Italy had begun to pursue a more non-interventionist policy even though light tanks and aircraft continued to flow into Spain until October 1936.[6] After British diplomats had convinced French leaders that intervention in Spain, even sending supplies, was dangerous, the French proposed that the policy of non-intervention be legitimated through some form of committee on the 2nd of August.[7] To the British preventing any further intervention would localize the conflict. Eden therefore put an embargo on Spain in August 1936 hoping it would 'induce… Germany and Italy to follow suit…' in effect limiting their aid.[8]

However, this matter was complicated by Soviet intervention in October 1936 as the Soviets began to supply the Republic with arms and light tanks.[9] By November 1936 the infamous German Condor Legion had been sent to Spain and Italy had sent in over 100 aircraft.[10] This looked like the build-up for a possible ideological conflict erupting in Spain and now made it imperative that the war be limited. Therefore the Non-Intervention Committee 'debarred states and private enterprises from providing aid to either side in the Spanish Civil War'.[11] Britain continued to pursue its policy of non-intervention in direct reaction to increased German and Italian intervention.

While overtly the goal of the Non-Intervention Committee was for all the powers that signed it (including the USSR, Germany and Italy) to have no intervention, there was tacit acknowledgment it could not adhere to this. Eden stated that it was 'tattered and full of holes no doubt, but better than total war in Spain, a European war out of that'.[12] The shift from merely a policy of non-intervention to attempting to bring other nations into a policy of non-intervention suggests the goal was to prevent the Axis from intervening to a large extent. As the committee had no international laws behind it, it allowed German or Italian aid to be sent there covertly and therefore at low levels. Germany and Italy could break the rules only to the extent to which the British were content their interests would not be impacted. This policy was directly focused at preventing the Axis from intervening as the committee came about not long after the escalation by the Axis, as both the timing and rhetoric of that time suggest.

Eden's memoirs, *Facing the Dictators*, have been frequently cited in arguments about the different factors of appeasement which influenced British policy within this essay; thus determining the value and limitations of this source will have implications for the strength of this evidence.

---

5 *ibid.*

6 Forrest, *op. cit.*, pg. 71.

7 Preston, *op. cit.*, pg. 141.

8 Manchester, W., 1988, *The Last Lion: Winston Spencer Churchill, alone 1932–1940*, London: Little, Brown and Company, pg. 201.

9 Forrest, *op. cit.*, pg. 71.

10 Forrest, *op. cit.*, pg. 71.

11 Graham, H., 2005, *The Spanish Civil War: A very short introduction*, New York: Oxford University Press, pg. 38.

12 Eden, *op. cit.*, pg. 466.

Eden was the British foreign minister from 1935 to 1938 as well as serving in the Foreign Office before this period, making his memoirs a valuable source.[13] As foreign minister he was responsible for meeting with foreign leaders and a key adviser in cabinet meetings of the British government to decide foreign policies. Therefore, his views of the Spanish conflict as well as his reasoning are valuable in examining the reasons for British foreign policy. His view of Spain as anachronistic and that war must be averted at any cost are clear from his memoirs and this view would have been passed to the British cabinet. It is therefore Eden as the origin of the source that makes it valuable for my question.

Most of the memoirs were written based on personal letters, official letters and official documents that he either possessed or requested, which suggests Eden has information from all offices of the British foreign service and therefore would be able to provide exhaustive details for all British agencies.[14] He would also have the many documents that the foreign office wrote at the time which means he has information from the key intelligence and Spanish specialists. This makes the source valuable in helping us understand what the British foreign office thought of the crisis as well as the justification for its policy decisions.

However, the source was written in 1962, decades after the conflict when there was a whole new world order. The source may stress more ideological struggles because of the Cold War context or it may attempt to paint the author in a better light. Eden had retired from an unsuccessful time as prime minister and might have used these memoirs to point out previous successes. His failure during the Suez crisis could have led to him trying to paint himself as an astute diplomat. Therefore, the origin of the source being so close to his failure at Suez and there being a possible ulterior purpose suggest the source could be limited in understanding Eden's role in the Spanish crisis. This limits evidence garnered from the source for understanding Britain's role in the Spanish conflict.

---

13 Eden, A., 1962, *Facing the Dictators*, London: Cassell, pg. 1.
14 Eden, *op. cit.* pg. 1.

The vive voce

After you have handed in your essay, your supervisor will give you a short interview about your essay. This will last about 10–15 minutes and will give you the opportunity to talk about the writing process – what you found difficult, what you enjoyed and what you have learned – to share your passion for your topic, we would hope! It is also an opportunity for your supervisor to check for plagiarism.

The viva voce helps your supervisor to write his or her extended essay report on your essay. This in turn assists the IB examiner in rewarding the 'holistic' points for the essay, for example for your engagement with the process.

Plagiarism

As with the IA, you need to ensure that the extended essay is your own original work. If you are found to have plagiarized material to include in your essay you may well be disqualified from the IB Diploma Programme. Your supervisor may ask you to submit your extended essay via plagiarism-checking software.

Common problems

Problems with the research and writing process

- Students realize too late that there are not enough resources for their chosen topic.
- The focus of the question is not narrow enough.
- Students do not keep to deadlines and so do not benefit from constructive feedback from their supervisors.
- The writing process is left too late and is rushed at the end.
- Students do not check the marking criteria until after they have written the essay. Instead, refer to these at all stages of your writing.
- Students lose work on the computer. Keep back-ups!

Problems with the final extended essay

- The research question is not clearly set out in the introduction.
- School textbooks and/or general or inappropriate websites are used for research.
- There is poor referencing and/or bibliography.

Activity

Use the checklist below to ensure that you have covered all of the elements of the extended essay.

Extended essay component	Checked ✓
Title page	
Abstract	
Contents page	
Page numbers throughout	
Introduction	
Main body	
Evaluation of sources used	
Chapter headings	
Conclusion	
References	
Works cited listed in alphabetical order by author	
Appendices	

Here is an example of a full Extended essay. Examiner's comments are given throughout the essay and there is an evaluation and mark sheet at the end.

Extended essay

Name: Jo Smith

Candidate number: XXXXXXX

Topic: Danish resistance in the second world war

Research question: To what extent was the Danish Resistance Movement successful in disrupting the Nazi occupation of Denmark (1940–1945)?
Word count: 3,998

Abstract: To what extent was the Danish Resistance Movement successful in disrupting the Nazi occupation of Denmark (1940–1945)?

The main aim of this essay is to evaluate how successful the Danish Resistance Movement was in disrupting Nazi rule in Denmark between 1945 and its liberation in 1950. The essay explores the methods used by the Danes to cause havoc for their occupiers throughout the occupation. Firstly, the essay analyses the importance of national unity in being the key to causing strikes throughout the occupation. Strikes would prove to be fundamental in disrupting Nazi rule as they were one of the key reasons for the declaration of a state of emergency in 1944. Secondly, the essay evaluates the importance of the media, and communication with Britain, in disrupting Nazi rule. The essay goes on to discuss the different acts of sabotage performed by the resistance and evaluate how successful they were in disrupting Nazi rule. Finally, the essay finishes with the key event that disrupted Nazi rule, the evacuation of Danish Jews to Sweden.

The evidence discussed throughout the essay leads to the conclusion that the Danish Resistance Movement was successful in disrupting Nazi occupation in Denmark as the Nazis were forced to declare a state of emergency in 1944. The movement may not have managed to force the Nazis out, as liberation was brought about when Germany surrendered to the allies, but nevertheless the resistance made the occupation for the Nazis far from an easy task.

Contents

Introduction

Denmark was neutral throughout the first world war and supported the League of Nations in attempting to keep the peace between the European powers. However, the situation for the Danes in the Second World War would be very different. Despite having signed a non-aggression pact with Germany the year before, on 9 April 1940

The research question is clearly stated

Examiner's comment
Title page, page numbering and contents page are all included

The scope of the research question is described

The conclusion is stated

The research question is put into context

German troops attacked neutral Denmark. The Danish military was small as it was only intended for a position of neutrality and 'to prevent unnecessary sacrifice of life in an obviously losing cause.'[1] The King of Denmark, Christian X, called for cease fire[2] and with only 16 casualties[3] at the end of the day, Denmark became occupied by Hitler's Germany. As Denmark wasn't officially at war, life didn't change dramatically. Christian X and the Danish government agreed to 'co operation' with the Nazis and in turn the Nazis wouldn't intervene in Danish domestic affairs. By following the 'co operation policy' Denmark remained peaceful, being known as an 'exemplary protectorate'[4] in Berlin but as 'Hitler's Pet Canary'[5] by the Allies.

The significance of the topic is identified

Nevertheless, 'beneath this impeccable veneer of calm acceptance were boiling feelings of defiance against the occupation.'[6] Despite being slow in getting organized, starting with little acts of defiance, such as shunning all German salutes and giving them 'the cold shoulder', the resistance eventually became a national movement which involved the whole population. After 1943, the Danish resistance caused constant problems for their Nazi occupiers with bombings of factories, regular strikes, millions of resistance leaflets and newspapers such as *Frit Denmark* being published and the evacuation of their Jewish population to neutral Sweden. In the Germans' eyes 'Denmark caused us more difficulties than anything else.'[7]

Chapter 1: Strikes

Early resistance began as 'symbolic resistance' and this would carry on throughout the war as an undertone of protest. Symbols varied from allied flags to RAF caps, and lapel badges with inscriptions partly in Morse code translating into 'Denmark = Against Nazi-Denmark'.[8] In itself symbolic resistance caused little disruption but it was very successful in the sense that it brought the Danish population together as it symbolized national unity and rejection of Nazi rule. The uniting of the population led to 'another headache'[9] for the Nazis. The Danes went on strike against different parts of the Nazi regime that they greatly disagreed with as well as different laws that the Nazis passed or attempted to pass. Some were smaller strikes limited to particular groups of people but others united the entire population to stand up against their occupiers.

Clear chapter headings identify the key themes

The earliest strike that marked the first open protest against the government's policy of 'co operation' was the student protest against Denmark joining the Anti-Comintern Pact on 25 November 1941. Most Danes feared that the signing of the pact would mean that they would be considered official allies of the Axis powers. The demonstrators weren't supporters of communists, 'it was foremost a protest against the government policy of negotiation'.[10] The protest lasted for several days and even though it was supposed to be a peaceful protest the Danish police attacked the demonstrators. The shock of seeing Danish police beating and arresting fellow Danes was the beginning of active resistance for some.

'Union members with communists at the helm'[11] would lead the largest number of strikes throughout the summer of 1943, known as the August Uprisings. They began

---

1 Lande, D. A. *Resistance! Occupied Europe and its defiance of Hitler,* 2000, MBI Publishing Company, St. Paul, MN, p.52.
2 See Appendix.
3 Lande, D. A. *Resistance! Occupied Europe and its defiance of Hitler,* 2000, MBI Publishing Company, St. Paul, MN, p.52.
4 www.nationalmuseet.dk/graphics/danske/Frihedsmuseet/October1943-200_ml.pdf
5 www.holocaustresearchproject.org/revolt/danishresistance.html, Winston Churchill. Accessed 22 August 2009.
6 Lande, D. A. *Resistance! Occupied Europe and its defiance of Hitler,* 2000, MBI Publishing Company, St. Paul, MN, p.53.
7 www.nationalmuseet.dk/graphics/danske/Frihedsmuseet/October1943-200_ml.pdf Adolph Eichmann.
8 See Appendix.
9 Lande, D. A. *Resistance! Occupied Europe and its defiance of Hitler,* 2000, MBI Publishing Company, St. Paul, MN, p.60.
10 Levine, E. *Darkness over Denmark, The Danish resistance and the rescue of the Jews,* 2000, Holiday House, New York, p.32.
11 Kjeldbœk, E. *The Museum of Danish Resistance 1940–45,* published by the Museum of Danish Resistance, Copenhagen, p.23.

at a shipyard in Odense with shipyard workers dropping their tools and walking out when German troops marched in with guns. 'In an act of solidarity'[12] all the workers in every factory in Odense also walked out. The strikes in Odense were followed by clashes with the German authorities where several people were wounded when the Germans opened fire on the crowd. Strikes in other Danish towns such as Esbjerg also occurred where everyone in town including police, civil servants and other labourers walked out from their jobs. In an attempt to restore order the Germans enforced a curfew but had to lift it soon after as the people 'thronged to the streets leading to confrontations with the police and soldiers'.[13] The August Uprisings spread all the way from Aalborg over to Zealand. The strikes throughout the August Uprisings were key in disrupting Nazi rule in Denmark as they forced Best to demand a 'state of emergency' as 'Danish authorities had lost control of the strikes and demonstrations'.[14]

The largest and most successful strike of 1944 occurred when the Germans imposed a curfew from 8pm to 5am on 25 June 1944: the whole population of Copenhagen went on strike by not reporting for work. The Germans attempted to stop the strike by cutting off all food, water and electricity supplies to the city but nevertheless the strike continued. On 3 July '5,000 fires illuminated the streets during blackout hours'[15] which again was an act of protest against Nazi rule. Despite political leaders urging the strike to stop, it continued until 4 July 'as the leaders of the Resistance, the Freedom Council, urged a continuation until certain demands had been met'.[16] The strike was a huge success as the curfew was lifted and the much hated Schalburg Corps were removed from the streets. When Germans tried to deport Danish police Copenhagen went on strike a second time in the autumn and 'civilians flocked to the resistance movement and enrolment exceeded 45,000 at its largest point'.[17]

The strikes proved to be a very successful method of defying Nazi rule in Denmark. When they were organized and well coordinated the resistance managed to get the demands they wished for, which was seen in the Copenhagen strikes in 1944 when they demanded the removal of the imposed curfew. The strikes caused great havoc for the Nazis as due to the government not being able to control the strikes, Best had to declare a state of emergency. The Danes proved that by uniting and working together they managed to cause great distress to the Germans.

At the end of the chapter there is analysis of points and a link back to the research question

Chapter 2: Media and communication with Britain

In the early years of the occupation the resistance was not very well organized and therefore there was not a lot of violent resistance taking place against the Germans. There were, however, lots of different newspapers and pamphlets being printed in Denmark's illegal underground press, which roused resistance for the country's German occupiers and 'even established parties wished to have a voice in the illegal press'[18] in the final years of the war, showing the resistance's growing influence. The aim of the illegal newspapers was to communicate underground news and to 'foster an understanding for the resistance movement among the Danish population'.[19] The newspapers ranged from local to national and by the end of the occupation there

---

12 Lande, D. A. *Resistance! Occupied Europe and its defiance of Hitler,* 2000, MBI Publishing Company, St. Paul, MN, p.60.
13 Lande, D. A. *Resistance! Occupied Europe and its defiance of Hitler,* 2000, MBI Publishing Company, St. Paul, MN, p.60.
14 Kjeldbœk, E. *The Museum of Danish Resistance 1940–45,* published by the Museum of Danish Resistance, Copenhagen, p.23. See Appendix.
15 Lande, D. A. *Resistance! Occupied Europe and its defiance of Hitler,* 2000, MBI Publishing Company, St. Paul, MN, p.66.
16 The Museum of Danish Resistance under 'Folkestrejken 1944'.
17 www.holocaustresearchproject.org/revolt/danishresistance.html
18 The Museum of Danish Resistance under 'Illegal Presse'.
19 Kjeldbœk, E. *The Museum of Danish Resistance 1940–45,* published by the Museum of Danish Resistance, Copenhagen, p.11.

Has referred to appendices in the footnotes

were more than 530[20] illegal papers and 6.3 million copies[21] of one newspaper alone, *Frit Danmark*, were printed.

The newspapers were important as they encouraged acts of sabotage. The press became the centre for encouragement and praise for the work of the resistance, which kept morale high for the resistance and population. One issue of *Boycott* read 'the least we can do – and we all can – is to boycott the axis'[22] showing how the press encouraged the population to stand up and defy their Nazi occupiers. There were also other tabloids that angrily made Nazi 'calaborators' known to the rest of the Danish population. *Vaememagstens Damebekendtskaber* published the names of women who fraternized with German officers, calling them 'feltmaddraser – field mattresses',[23] while *Den Blaa Blogen* listed businesses who were working with the Nazis.

Precise evidence is given to support arguments

The underground press was successful in disrupting Nazi occupation as the Germans realized the success of the illegal newspapers and were therefore always trying to prevent their publication. Nazi officers would constantly search for the printing presses and the journalists who wrote the articles but as the printing of the newspapers was done in complete secret and in so many places it was very difficult to find them and therefore many copies were printed, keeping up morale throughout the occupation. These illegal newspapers are a useful source for showing the view of the Danish about the Nazi occupiers and the actions of the resistance, though as these publishers' primary aim was to keep Danish morale high, they may not have written about events when the resistance was unsuccessful and this is a limitation to using this source for this essay.

Has evaluated the sources being used for evidence

Contact with the Allies, in particular Britain, was a key to the success of the resistance movement. The BBC made broadcasts in Danish which the Danes would listen to, their own radios being filled with German propaganda. Despite the Germans' attempts to jam the signals from Britain, the Danes were able to listen and stay in contact with Britain throughout the war.

The key role that Britain played in helping the resistance was that 'Fra 1943 nedkastede SOE sabotageudstyr og våben til modstandsbevægelsen'.[24] Communication with Britain and being able to listen to broadcasts were key as the BBC would broadcast 'code words in the form of nonsensical phrases to tip them off to arms drops and other covert activity'.[25] Many Danes lent their houses to the underground signallers. This was very dangerous because if they were caught by Germans they would face imprisonment or deportation to concentration camps.

The British made many successful arms drops in the last years of the war. The first took place on 11 March 1943 and more followed but it was in August 1944 when 'more than 95% of the total amount of equipment received was dropped'.[26] Using British bombers, arms would be dropped in huge containers which took many men to carry. Therefore, the area where containers would be dropped had to be known exactly as it took a lot of effort to carry them to safety before they were spotted by the Germans.

By keeping contact with Britain the resistance gravely defied Nazi rule. The supply of British weapons in the last years allowed for more successful and larger sabotage attacks. The broadcasts were important in keeping the Danish population informed

---

20 Levine, E. *Darkness over Denmark, The Danish resistance and the rescue of the Jews*, 2000, Holiday House, New York, p.36.

21 Lande, D. A. *Resistance! Occupied Europe and its defiance of Hitler*, 2000, MBI Publishing Company, St. Paul, MN, p.53.

22 Lande, D. A. *Resistance! Occupied Europe and its defiance of Hitler*, 2000, MBI Publishing Company, St. Paul, MN, pp.54–55.

23 The Museum of Danish Resistance under 'The 'whipped cream front'.

24 www.natmus.dk/sw4607.asp. Translation from 1943 – the SOE dropped sabotage gear and weapons to the resistance.

25 Lande, D. A. *Resistance! Occupied Europe and its defiance of Hitler*, 2000, MBI Publishing Company, St. Paul, MN, p.55.

26 Kjeldbœk, E. *The Museum of Danish Resistance 1940–45*, published by the Museum of Danish Resistance, Copenhagen, p.19.

3

about war events. Many Danish officials had fled to England before the war and were communicating and helping the resistance from London headquarters. Communicating with Britain also meant that Danes were able to train there and would later be dropped and parachuted into Denmark, performing the earliest acts of sabotage.

Chapter 3: Sabotage

Sabotage proved to be the most effective method to disrupt Nazi rule in Denmark. It became much more effective and a real problem for the Nazis after arms drops where the Danes received weapons from Britain. Early sabotage started in 1942 and was mainly done by 'boy's groups' such the Churchill Club from Aalborg (who were all caught and executed in May 1942) and groups made up of members from the illegal communist party using homemade weapons. As the occupation continued, more groups from the resistance carried out sabotage throughout Denmark, concentrating on hitting the industrial sector.

The Communist Party formed the earliest sabotage groups, performing small-scale sabotage in the beginning of the occupation using homemade firebombs and later stolen explosives from Danish stockpiles. Most of the saboteurs had had previous experience as volunteers in the Spanish civil war in the 1930s, which proved to be very helpful in the fight against their occupiers. The communist sabotage leader in Copenhagen, Eigil Larsen, produced the 'cook book' manual for sabotage[27] showing how to make homemade bombs which was used by his fellow saboteurs. They also performed the first railway sabotage where they 'derailed a north going German ammunition-train'[28] in Northern Zealand. The damage done by the saboteurs in 1942 was minor yet 'the Germans' reaction would prove sabotage to be one of the main problems underlying the Dano-German relationship'.[29]

The number of sabotage missions greatly increased in 1943, reaching 220 by the end of August[30], mainly hitting armament factories and businesses. Danish factories, machine works, shipyards and small businesses all helped with the German war effort and it was businesses like these that were hit. There were 2,600 sabotage actions in all.[31] The resistance group Borgelige Partisaner (BOPA) had many members who were or had been apprentices in large factories and this proved useful in identifying targets which were supplying the German military. There were many acts of sabotage on arms factories such as Burmeister, Wain and Riffelsyndikatet in 1943, Riffelsyndikatet (again) and Global in 1944 and Always in 1945. The Riffle Syndicate produced the Madsen machine guns and 20mm cannon and this sabotage act 'was the most extensive caused by sabotage in Denmark'.[32] In order for BOPA members to recognize each other they wore white scarves during their sabotage of the Globus factory.

Sabotage acts continued and on 28 July 1943 the German Minelayer LINZ was hit. Danskernes modstandslegender[33], Citronen and Flammen were key members in the resistance group Holger Danske and altogether 'gennemførte de 11 drab'.[34] On 24 August 1943 they played a pivotal role in what would be the trigger for the Nazis to declare a 'state of emergency' in Denmark when they blew the Forum, the largest public hall in Copenhagen, to smithereens. They cleverly hid the explosions in a

27 See Appendix.
28 The Museum of Danish resistance under 'Early sabotage 1942'.
29 Kjeldbœk, E. *The Museum of Danish Resistance 1940–45,* published by the Museum of Danish Resistance, Copenhagen, p.14.
30 Lande, D. A. *Resistance! Occupied Europe and its defiance of Hitler,* 2000, MBI Publishing Company, St. Paul, MN, p.56.
31 Kjeldbœk, E. *The Museum of Danish Resistance 1940–45,* published by the Museum of Danish Resistance, Copenhagen, p.22.
32 The Museum of Danish resistance under 'Industrial sabotage 1943–44'.
33 www.natmus.dk/sw54418.asp translation – the Danish resistance legends.
34 www.natmus.dk/sw54420.asp translation – were involved in 11 sabotage acts.

4

Clear conclusion to the chapter linking back to the research question

Introductory paragraphs to each chapter clearly set out the argument of the chapter and link to the research question

Precise evidence is given to support arguments

Carlsberg beer crate.[35] The sabotage on the Forum was a key breakthrough in the fight against the Nazis as it was the trigger to the Germans calling a 'state of emergency' demanding the government introduce the death penalty for saboteurs. However, the Danish government rejected the ultimatum.

Finally, in the last years of the war, the freedom council sent saboteurs down to Jutland 'as Germans desperately attempted to dispatch reinforcements to the battle of Ardennes'.[36] They blew up the railways, which caused more than 1,500 interruptions[37] lasting from hours to days, delaying the German reinforcements for a total of three days. The resistance movement believed the more Germans were in Denmark the fewer there were to fight the battles in France.

Sabotage caused constant disturbances for Nazi rule as in the end it was sabotage that forced them to declare a state of emergency as disturbances were disrupting the Nazi occupation so much. The blowing up of arms factories slowed down weapon production for the German military, and the exploding of railways and bridges caused great disturbances to German communication and transportation.

There is a clear conclusion to the chapter linking back to the research question

Chapter 4: The evacuation of the Danish Jews

The most successful operation carried out by the Danish resistance, which hugely disrupted the Nazi occupation in Denmark, was the defiance of the Nazi plans of 'the final solution' for Danish Jews. The Danes' success in saving their Jewish population from certain death from the Nazis came from helping Danish Jews into hiding and eventually evacuating 95% of them to Sweden.

Indicates the line of argument in the opening sentence

The source *Darkness over Denmark* by Ellen Levine was particularly useful for this section of the essay as it includes biographies of people who experienced the occupation, some of whom took part in this evacuation of the Jews. However, as Levine carried out her interviews many years after the war, it is possible that some of the information in this book is inaccurate or exaggerated by people who wanted to make the occupation seem worse than it actually was.

Includes an analysis of sources used

The Jewish population of Denmark lived freely under German occupation up until late 1942 when anti-Semitic acts started by Nazi soldiers such as 'painting swastikas on the walls of Copenhagen synagogue'[38] and plans to carry out 'the final solution' on the Jewish Danes started. King Christian X said, 'There is no Jewish question in this country. There is only my people.'[39] Hitler, however, found the freedom of the Danish Jews 'loathsome' and was enraged when Danish police defended the Jews.

When a military state of emergency was declared on 29 August 1943, Best wrote to Hitler that he 'intend[ed] to govern the Danes with a heavy hand'[40] and sent a telegram to Berlin saying 'the time has come to turn our attention to the solution of the Jewish question.'[41] Hitler formally approved a plan for the deportation of the 8,000 Jewish Danes. 'The final solution' had reached Denmark.

Best believed that the Danes would resist by a general strike and provoke 'a cessation of all cooperation from Danish governmental bodies'[42] in order to protect their Jewish population. He requested extra police from Berlin, believing it was necessary

---

35 See Appendix.
36 Lande, D. A. *Resistance! Occupied Europe and its defiance of Hitler*, 2000, MBI Publishing Company, St. Paul, MN, p.67.
37 Lande, D. A. *Resistance! Occupied Europe and its defiance of Hitler*, 2000, MBI Publishing Company, St. Paul, MN, p.67.
38 Lande, D. A. *Resistance! Occupied Europe and its defiance of Hitler*, 2000, MBI Publishing Company, St. Paul, MN, p.57.
39 Lande, D. A. *Resistance! Occupied Europe and its defiance of Hitler*, 2000, MBI Publishing Company, St. Paul, MN, p.57.
40 www.nationalmuseet.dk/graphics/danske/Frihedsmuseet/October1943-200_ml.pdf
41 www.nationalmuseet.dk/graphics/danske/Frihedsmuseet/October1943-200_ml.pdf
42 Levine, E. *Darkness over Denmark, The Danish resistance and the rescue of the Jews*, 2000, Holiday House, New York, p.65.

if they were going to round up all the Jews in one go. Gestapo agents, additional German SS troops and men from the office of Jewish affairs arrived in Denmark. A German police battalion was set up under Dr Rudolf Midner, leader of the political department at Auschwitz, and later two ships arrived which would be used to deport Jews to Theresienstadt concentration camp in Czechoslovakia. Most Jews still believed that the Germans would bring them no harm as Best and Svenningsen confirmed that the Jewish communities were in no danger. However, Georg F. Duckwitz, a close friend of the Social Democrats party, was informed of the round-up of the Danish Jews by Best and quickly informed the social democrats of the Nazis' intentions saying, 'the disaster is here! Everything is planned in detail.'[43] The democrats quickly informed Jewish leaders, who told their people the next morning that they had to go into immediate hiding. Non-Jewish Danes spread the news of the planned raids as many who weren't involved in the resistance joined. By being a united nation and spreading the news quickly, the Danish resistance prevented a successful round-up of the Jews on the night between 1 October and 2 October 1943. It was a huge blow to Best and the Nazi plans as nearly 95% of the Jews[44] had gone into hiding. The Nazis only managed to capture 284[45] Jews out of 8,000. Adolph Eichmann, organizer of the deportation of the Danish Jews, was extremely annoyed by the fiasco saying, 'Denmark caused us more difficulties than anything else.'[46]

Thousands of Danes were now hiding Jews in their churches, attics, country homes and residences to wait for a safe passage across the sea to Sweden. Due to the Danish population being protective of their Jewish population, believing that 'det vaerste de(Tyskarna) endnu har bagaaet'[47] and 'forbavselsen kan vi ikke deltage i'[48], many Danes felt the need to help the Jews by conveying warnings and finding hiding places, food and transportation to the coast. Hospitals in Copenhagen were also vital transit stations. The hospitals would hide the Jews in rooms for staff or Jews were admitted with fictitious ailments. During the October Days 2,000[49] Jews passed though Bispebjerg Hospital. As historian Lenil Yahil said, 'a living wall raised by the Danish people in one night protected their country men'[50] and therefore very few Jews were caught or betrayed while in hiding, making it extremely difficult for the Nazis.

The resistance disrupted the Nazi plan even further and the 'Danish population as a whole became an instrument of defiance'[51] when the Danes organized the successful evacuation of the Jews to Sweden. These evacuations departed from various harbours along the coast as well as some open beaches.[52] Fishermen took a huge risk helping the Jews, facing imprisonment and forfeiture of their boats if caught taking them to Sweden as well as the danger of crossing a sea full of mines. The movement organized the evacuation as well as finding means for financing the procedure; most money came from wealthy Danes who wanted to play their part. Resistant leader Jorgen Kieler told the resistance, 'Money and boats, that's what we need'.[53] The Jews were

---

43 Levine, E. *Darkness over Denmark, The Danish resistance and the rescue of the Jews*, 2000, Holiday House, New York, p.68.
44 Levine, E. *Darkness over Denmark, The Danish resistance and the rescue of the Jews*, 2000, Holiday House, New York, p.73.
45 Lande, D. A. *Resistance! Occupied Europe and its defiance of Hitler*, 2000, MBI Publishing Company, St. Paul, MN, p.64.
46 www.nationalmuseet.dk/graphics/danske/Frihedsmuseet/October1943-200_ml.pdf
47 www.befrielsen1945.dk/temaer/samarbejdemodstand/modstand/kilder/fd1943.pdf. p.3. Translation - the worst the Germans have done up till now.
48 www.befrielsen1945.dk/temaer/samarbejdemodstand/modstand/kilder/fd1943.pdf. p.3. Translation - this we can't be a part of.
49 www.nationalmuseet.dk/graphics/danske/Frihedsmuseet/October1943-200_ml.pdf
50 Levine, E. *Darkness over Denmark, The Danish resistance and the rescue of the Jews*, 2000, Holiday House, New York, p.74. Quoted in Lenil Yahil, *The Rescue of Danish Jewry*, 1984, Jewish Publication Society of America, Philadelphia, PA, p.188.
51 Lande, D. A. *Resistance! Occupied Europe and its defiance of Hitler*, 2000, MBI Publishing Company, St. Paul, MN, p.66.
52 See Appendix.
53 Levine, E. *Darkness over Denmark, The Danish resistance and the rescue of the Jews*, 2000, Holiday House, New York, p.80.

6

transported across the sea to Sweden by many different methods, some in large fishing boats, others in small kayaks and rowboats. The elderly and young were also smuggled inside freight cars on the regular ferries between Denmark and Sweden.

Gilleleje was a very important escape route: in total about one fifth[54] of the Danish Jews escaped from here. However, 'October's greatest tragedy'[55] took place here as the Gestapo were suspicious of the busy activity in the harbours on the first few days of the evacuation (1 October and 2 October) and, on 6 October, 80 Jews were betrayed by a Danish girl in love with a German officer and were rounded up by the Gestapo when hiding in the attic of the church. The resistance moved the operations to smaller more remote places along the coast as all further sailing from Gilleleje was impossible.

The evacuation of the Danish Jews was a huge success. In total only 481[56] out of 8,000 were rounded up and sent to the concentration camp in Czechoslovakia[57] and at the end of the war Denmark had one of the lowest statistical casualty rates for Jews in the war due to the coordination and commitment of the Danish nation and resistance against their Nazi occupiers. The resistance delayed Hitler's plan for the Jewish population and in the end even went so far as to prevent it completely. The evacuation also benefited the resistance in the long run as the Danes had made contacts and a whole illegal network of service routes was developed, including The Danish-Swedish Refugee Service. This was notably the Danish resistance's biggest achievement in defying and disrupting Nazi rule.

There is a clear link back to the research question at the end of the chapter

Conclusion

The surrender of Germany in Denmark was announced on the BBC news in Danish on 4 May 1945 at 8.35pm, and become effective on 5 May at 8am. The Danish resistance itself did not cause the surrender of the Germans as it was the victory of the allies that forced Germany to surrender Denmark. Nevertheless, the Danish Resistance Movement was successful throughout the five-year occupation in disrupting Nazi rule. The Danes refused to be seen as being official allies of Germany and caused havoc for their occupiers throughout the years, reaching a peak in 1943 when Best declared a state of emergency.

Links back to the research question and answers it. Consistent with the evidence in the essay.

The Danes used all the methods they could to cause disturbances for the Nazis whether they were violent methods, like constant sabotage of industries or strikes which led to violence with the German troops, or peaceful methods, such as publishing millions of pamphlets and newspapers. They used their proximity to Sweden to great effect, managing to evacuate nearly all their Jewish population there by sea. The support for the allies that the resistance showed throughout the occupation caused disruption for the Nazis to a great extent too: it was the equipment from Britain that supplied the saboteurs with weapons as well as being used to train men who would later parachute into Denmark to help with the resistance.

At the end of the second world war Denmark was officially recognized as one of the Allies by the rest of the world. The Danes had primarily received this title due to the nationalistic movement of the resistance in denying their occupier's rule by causing disturbances for the Nazis throughout the war[58]. Half of the Danish post-war government were key representatives of the resistance[59], showing that they had a huge impact not only on the Nazi occupation but also in rebuilding post-war Denmark.

---

54 www.nationalmuseet.dk/graphics/danske/Frihedsmuseet/October1943-200_ml.pdf
55 www.nationalmuseet.dk/graphics/danske/Frihedsmuseet/October1943-200_ml.pdf
56 Lande, D. A. *Resistance! Occupied Europe and its defiance of Hitler,* 2000, MBI Publishing Company, St. Paul, MN, p.65.
57 See Appendix.
58 Translated from Weibull, J. *Böckers Lexicon,* 1984, Bokförlaget Bra Böcker AB Höganäs, p.194.
59 Translated from *Nationalencyklopedin Fjärde Bandet Bokförlaget Bra Böcker,* 1990, Bokförlaget Bra Böcker AB Höganäs.

Appendices

Below are only examples of the appendices included in this essay.

Appendices are referred to in the footnotes, making their inclusion in the essay relevant

1 Clash between a non-commissioned German officer and a crowd in Ålborg, 24 August 1943

The Museum of Danish Resistance under 'Symbolsk modstand'

2 The different routes used to evacuate the Jews from the Danish coasts to the Swedish coasts

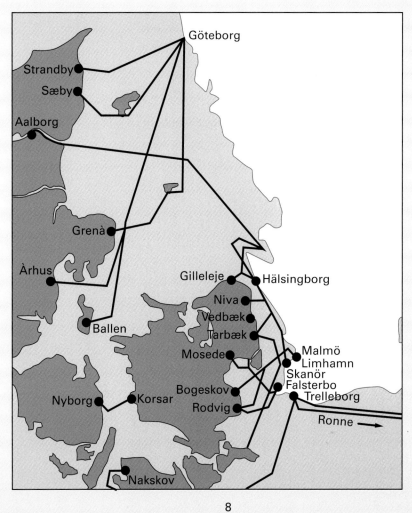

Bibliography

Museum
- The Museum of Danish Resistance

  Churchillparken

  DK-1263 Copenhagen K

  Denmark

Books
- Kjeldbœk, E. (1990) *The Museum of Danish Resistance 1940–45*, published by The Museum of Danish Resistance, Copenhagen.

- Lande, D. A. (2000) *Resistance! Occupied Europe and its defiance of Hitler,* MBI Publishing Company, St Paul, MN.

- Levine, E. (2000) *Darkness over Denmark, The Danish resistance and the rescue of the Jews,* Holiday House, New York.

- Weibull, J. (1984) *Bra Böckers Lexicon,* Bokförlaget Bra Böcker AB Höganäs

Encyclopaedias
- *Nationalencyklopedin Fjärde Bandet Bokförlaget Bra Böcker* (1990) Bokförlaget Bra Böcker AB Höganäs

Websites
- www.befrielsen1945.dk/temaer/samarbejdemodstand/modstand/kilder/fd1943.pdf

  Accessed 27 August 2009

- www.historylearningsite.co.uk/danish_resistance.htm

  Accessed 5 July 2009

- www.holocaustresearchproject.org/revolt/danishresistance.html

  Accessed 10 July 2009

- www.nationalmuseet.dk/graphics/danske/Frihedsmuseet/October1943-200_ml.pdf

  Accessed 29 August 2009

- www.natmus.dk/sw4607.asp

  Accessed 2 September 2009

- www.natmus.dk/sw54418.asp

  Accessed 21 August 2009

Footnotes and referencing are set out in acceptable and consistent format

9

Overall assessment

	Criterion	Mark	Maximum	Comments
A	Research question	2	2	Clearly stated and sharply focused.
B	Introduction	2	2	All elements are included.
C	Investigation	3	4	A range of sources is used, including museum, primary and secondary and Internet sources. Possibly could do with a greater number of sources though. Thorough planning evident.
D	Knowledge and understanding	4	4	A thorough understanding of the topic is shown.
E	Reasoned argument	4	4	The argument is presented logically and clearly – a range of factors is presented leading through to the most significant factor in support of the argument in the final chapter.
F	Analysis and evaluation	3	4	Each chapter analyses the evidence rather than just describing it –and links continuously back to the overall research question. There is some evaluation of the evidence used.
G	Use of subject language	4	4	Appropriate language relevant to the topic is used and the ideas of the essay are communicated clearly.
H	Conclusion	2	2	This links back to the research question and is consistent with the evidence presented
I	Formal presentation	4	4	All aspects of presentation are covered.
J	Abstract	2	2	It contains the research question, its scope and the conclusion of the essay.
K	Holistic judgement	3	4	This is a less well-explored topic and the student has showed initiative in visiting the resistance museum in Denmark and in putting together a convincing argument with the evidence she has researched.

Total out of 36 marks: 33

6   Revision skills

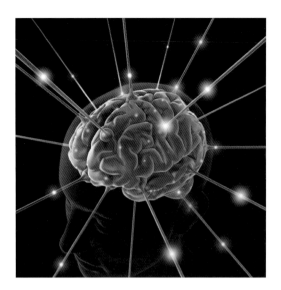

After completing an enjoyable, enlightening and rewarding two-year IB Diploma Programme history course, you have to be able to demonstrate your history skills in 5 hours of examination if you are an HL student or 2.5 hours if you are an SL student. It is vitally important that you maximize your potential by following a well planned out programme of revision. This should enable you to effectively revise the vast amount of material that you have covered over the two years, and to commit it to your long-term memory so that it can be used and applied relevantly in the examination.

Yes, there is no way round it – revising is tough, and for many students difficult and dull. However, you **have** to do it, and no one can learn the material for you. So how **do** you revise?

Have a plan: check what you need to know

You should begin by answering the following questions.

- Which Paper 1 prescribed subject have I studied?
- Which Paper 2 topics have I studied?
- Which regional Paper 3 am I taking, and which three sections have I studied?

Map out the content you will need to cover for each paper. See the example below (where the chart has been only started).

The overview content table

Paper 1	Prescribed subject 3	Brezhnev's domestic policies	Deng's economic policies	
Paper 2	Topic 3	Kenyatta	Peron	Hitler
	Topic 5	Wartime conferences	Truman Doctrine and Marshall Plan	
Paper 3	Section 5	Alexander II	Alexander III	
	Section 8	Germany 1919–1933	Italy 1919–1939	
	Section 9	Stalin 1924–1953	Great patriotic war	

Once you have mapped out an overview of the content, shade in areas that 'overlap'. For example, in route 2, prescribed subject 3, the section on Brezhnev to Gorbachev overlaps with Paper 3 section 9. Some of this material also is useful for answering an essay question on the end of the Cold War on Paper 2 topic 5. Mapping out the content you will need to cover in your revision helps you to better understand the 'big picture' of the material you have studied, and should also help you to make connections between topics.

This content table should clearly set down what you need to know for each examination paper. Do not try to pre-empt what will be on the paper. Do not leave out any topics or 'bullets' from specific sections. You need to know your way around the material and be sufficiently confident to draw only relevant information into your responses. Remember that examiners are paid to ask about the content differently and the test is designed to make you 'think on your feet'. You should not expect to see questions you have answered before, or to regurgitate a pre-planned essay.

Your revision plan needs to be drawn up well in advance so that you can begin revising at least six weeks before your examination. The revision timetable is designed to ensure that coverage of all subjects is complete before the examination. You should leave **some** blank time slots for 'emergencies', for example when an unplanned event comes up, or if there is an area of the course that you need to seek help with. Remember that the key to revision is to do it little and often. Take regular breaks after 45 minutes or an hour. Do not attempt 'marathon' sessions of four or more hours without a break. This can overload your brain, it is not effective for retaining lots of information in the longer term and it can stress you out!

Revision timetable 1

You should start revising six to eight weeks before the IB examination. Revision timetable 1 (below) is for revision **during** the last month or few weeks of school.

Day/Date	Morning session	Afternoon session	Evening session	Notes
Monday	*School/classes*	*School/classes*	1 hour biology: topic X 30–45 minutes history: topic – Causes of WW1	Incomplete Ask teacher re. role of 'imperial rivalries'
Tuesday	*School/classes*	*School/classes*	1 hour maths: topic Y 30–45 minutes: Spanish vocab	Ask teacher for extra help with these equations
Wednesday	*School/classes*	*School/classes*	1 hour English: 1984 Go to movies	
Thursday	*School/classes*	*School/classes*	1 hour music: topic B 30–45 minutes biology: topic C	
Friday	*School/classes*	*School/classes*	1 hour history: topic – Course of WW1 30–45 minutes maths: topic D	
Saturday	1 hour Spanish Break 1 hour English	1 hour music Break 1 hour biology	Go to birthday party!	
Sunday	1 hour history Break 1 hour maths	Go to watch football match	1 hour Spanish Break 1 hour English	

Revision timetable 2

Timetable 2 (below) is for the holidays just before the examination and for study leave. You will need to give more time to your HL subjects than your SL ones.

Day/Date	Morning session	Afternoon session	Evening session	Notes
Monday	1 hour history Break 1 hour biology	1 hour music Break 30–45 minutes Spanish Go shopping	45 minutes maths Break 45 minutes English	Need to cover more sub-topics for history next session
Tuesday				
Wednesday				
Thursday				
Friday				
Saturday				
Sunday				

Remember, you must take breaks, and have proper 'down time'. You should specify times when you will chat to friends, go out for a meal, watch a movie – basically do what you enjoy doing to relax. If you build this time into your revision plan then you will be able to have some non-study time without worrying about it. In other words, you need to set targets and give yourself little rewards. Meet your targets for each day and you will deserve some rewards!

Before you finalize your schedule or timetable make sure that you have covered sufficient topics in your revision.

Do you know enough to be able to answer the Paper 1 questions, two essays on Paper 2 and three essays on Paper 3?

Activity

Find examples of Papers 2 and 3 from the last three years. Go through these past papers and check that your revision will allow you to answer the correct number of essays and that you have will have enough choice.

Make good revision notes

You need to consider not only range but also depth. You need to make sure that you cover your chosen topics in enough detail so that you can provide the necessary level of evidence and analysis in **your essays to support any** arguments you make. The quality of your revision notes is therefore very important.

> How can I know what
> I think until I see what I say?
> E. M. FORSTER

Four step-plan

Step 1: Creating notes

Create and learn your own time lines and fact files. You need to know the chronology of events, what happened, when and who was significant.

Consolidate your class notes into revision notes (see below for ideas on how to do this). You should underline or highlight anything you are unsure about. If you find that you still do not fully understand a topic or part of a topic you should seek clarification from your teacher (or a reliable and capable friend).

Step 2: Adding depth

Synthesize historiography – you should only bring in the specific analysis of historians to your arguments when you fully understand how to analyse the material yourself. You should use historians' accounts as evidence in your arguments and not replace your analysis with vague summaries of their opinions.

Attempt to add depth in terms of the **details** you recall for each topic – key events, dates and statistics.

Step 3: Application

Practise past essay questions so that you understand how to apply appropriately and effectively the material you have learned. Doing this should also make it clear where the gaps in your knowledge lie. Draw up plans and/or write essays out in full, under timed conditions.

You should also create your own 'IB style' document and essay questions. You should have the curriculum details to hand so you can properly understand what possible questions could be asked about the material you have learned.

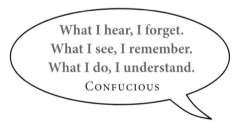

What I hear, I forget.
What I see, I remember.
What I do, I understand.
Confucious

Step 4: Continual review

Rereading and reviewing your notes is critical. You need familiarity with the material in order to be able to rework and manipulate the content to come up with essay plans in the examination. The more you go over your revision notes, the more you will be able to commit your notes to long-term memory.

Strategies for making revision notes

Here are some suggested strategies for making your revision notes meaningful.

Personalization

Personalize your revision notes. Manipulate the material, use colour codes and visuals. Indeed, visual learners might want to encode their notes with pictures or photos. The more creative you are with your revision notes the more likely it is that the information in them will be stored in your long-term memory.

Using time lines

These are an excellent way of sorting out chronology and helping you to understand the importance of different events. A time line can also be manipulated to help you analyse different issues. The following activities should give you some idea of how you can do this.

Activity

Task 1

Complete the following time line on Alexander II. Place key events above or below the time line to indicate the level of reform or repression that existed in each year.

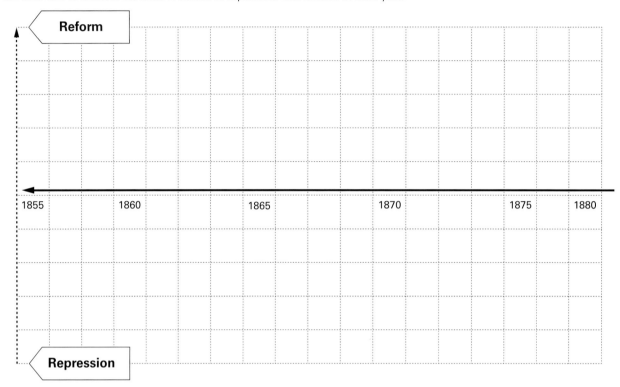

Task 2

Draw a time line of the Cold War from 1945 to 1989.

- Note the actions of the United States in one colour and the actions of the Soviet Union in another colour.

- Along the top of the page (but linked to the time line) write the US presidents' names; along the bottom of the page write the Soviet presidents' names.

- Shade the time line in different colours to indicate when the following periods in the Cold War took place:

> the breakdown of the Grand Alliance
>
> the Cold War goes global
>
> dangerous confrontation
>
> détente
>
> the second Cold War
>
> the collapse of the Soviet Union.

(You may be able to come up with more interesting or relevant headings for your time line.)

Using grids

Organizing your information in different ways is very important. Grids can help you to look at your knowledge in a thematic way and also help you see links between topics more easily.

Activity

Complete the following grids on the Vietnam War.

US presidents' policies in Vietnam

	Truman	Eisenhower	Kennedy	Johnson	Nixon
Situation in Vietnam					
Actions taken					
Successes					
Failures					
Overall legacy					

The different armies involved in Vietnam

	US Army	Viet Cong	ARVN
Who?			
Tactics used			
Key weaponry			
Morale			
Relationship with Vietnamese			

Mind mapping

For visual learners, drawing up spider diagrams or mind maps of each topic is a valuable exercise. Look back to page 15 to see an example of how you can do this.

Using revision cards

Once you have drawn up your revision notes, you may want to condense topics onto revision cards. These can be easily carried around and also have the advantage of allowing you to prioritize and reorder your notes easily. Consider writing a question on the front and putting the key points to the answer on the back of the card. This will allow you to test yourself easily – or make it easy for other people to test you.

Memorizing your notes

Memorizing information is key to your success. There is no 'quick fix' to learning the material. You will need to commit information to memory at least five times before it will move from your short-term memory to be stored in your long-term memory. While revising you must **do** something with the material which will help it to stay in your long-term memory. Just sitting on your bed or at a desk reading through pages and pages of notes will not be the most effective way of retaining the information. Write it down, quiz yourself and rewrite information differently, for example thematically rather than chronologically. Writing the material down is a key tool in your revision.

Testing yourself after each topic or sub-topic is important. You can turn over your notes and then test to see how much you have retained by reciting points out loud, or writing the key ideas and details down again.

What works best for me?

If you are a **visual learner** you could try the following strategies:

- Rewrite your notes as mind maps.
- Make illustrated diagrams of your notes.
- Use different colours to highlight different themes or to indicate change and continuity.

If you understand and remember information better when you hear or say it – in other words if you are an **auditory learner** – you could try the following strategies:

- Read your notes out loud.
- Make a sound recording of key events, dates and ideas which you can then listen to.
- Revise with other students, test each other orally and discuss key issues.
- Find different songs or tunes you like and substitute the lyrics for the main points of a topic.

If you prefer using **reading and writing** to learn you could try the following strategies:

- Copy and re-copy your notes, attempting to condense the content each time.
- Review your notes in silence, and usually alone.
- Write down the key points from memory.

You might discover that you learn best when you are being active. If so, you could try the following strategies:

- Review notes and rewrite them.
- Go through the main points from memory while jogging or swimming.

Most students find that a mixture of the approaches suggested above have the best results:

read it/see it – speak it/sing it/chant it – hear it – repeat it!

Mnemonics are often used effectively by teachers, and they are certainly worth experimenting with. A mnemonic is a 'sentence' or phrase that you devise as a tool to help you to remember a complex sequence of events or themes.

For example, taking the example of Germany's foreign policy, 1870–1914:

By **W**ednesday **M**ore **W**eeds **B**ack!

Bismarck's system – **W**eltpolitik – **M**oroccan Crises – **W**ar Council – **B**lank cheque

Alternatively, you could make up short poems of key words to help you to remember, or change the words of a favourite song into time lines and thematic sequences relevant to a topic you have studied.

Positive environment

You need to revise in a comfortable and quiet space. You should not listen to music, nor have your computer on for social networking, etc. Switch off your phone and let your family know you will need to be left in peace!

It is important that you maintain a healthy body to facilitate your learning. This means eating properly, taking breaks and getting enough sleep. To function effectively your brain needs 7 to 8 hours sleep a night, so avoid the temptation of continuing your revision into the early hours and then getting up early the next day.

Have a look at this website, which shows Tony Buzan's top tips for improving your memory:

www.pearsoned.co.uk/bookshop/article.asp?item=924

Preparing for the examination

Do you know what to expect on the day of the examination?

Paper 1

You should be clear about these points.

- You will have 1 hour in which to answer four set questions.
- You need to know the broad topic of the paper.

- You will not know the specific topic or theme of the documents – but you should revise **all** the bullets in the curriculum document so that you understand the theme.
- You might not be familiar with every document on the paper or the names or events mentioned – but don't panic.
- Paper 1 tests your historical understanding and your ability to put documents into their historical context.
- Question 1 tests historical comprehension and interpretations.
- Question 2 tests analysis of comparisons and contrasts.
- Question 3 tests evaluation of origin and purpose for value and limitations.
- Question 4 tests essay writing and synthesis of your own knowledge along with the sources.

Make sure you have learned relevant material for each of the bullet points set for this paper. You should also practise planning mini-essay responses. As with the essay papers, think about the types of question you could be asked and plan out the content that you would need to include to support the sources.

Paper 2

You should be clear about these points.

- You will have 1 hour and 30 minutes to complete Paper 2 (45 minutes per essay)
- Each topic has six questions.
- You must do two questions – each one taken from a different topic.
- You should make comparisons and contrasts between case studies.
- You should have cross-regional examples.

Paper 3

You should be clear about these points.

- You have 2 hours and 30 minutes to complete Paper 3.
- You need to write three essays from a choice of 24.
- You can choose any three essays.
- You need detailed knowledge of your regional sections.

Finally...

- Always read through the questions carefully.
- Highlight the key words and terms.
- Answer the question that is on the paper, not the one you want to answer!
- Try to trust in your memory – you **will** be able to remember your material if you have followed a proper revision plan.

Good luck!

History theory of knowledge

Introduction

What's the point?

> Philosopher (loud and clear): Men cannot really know the past.
>
> Historian (stupidly): What did you say?
>
> Philosopher (irritably): I said, 'Men cannot really know the past', and you know damn well that's what I said…
>
> J. H. Hexter, History Primer

The most important justification for this section of the book is the belief that theory of knowledge (TOK) is very much at the heart of the IB programme. The principles of TOK of self-reflection and critical analysis, the questioning of how we can know anything – what philosophy calls **epistemology** – are valuable in and for themselves. However, as a busy history student you are probably also interested in more quantifiable outcomes of how TOK can make you a better history student who gets better grades.

epistemology: the study or a theory of the nature and grounds of knowledge, especially with reference to what can and cannot be known

TOK knowledge issues

Obviously, an interest in TOK issues in history will help you with your TOK presentation and essay. History is a privileged 'area of knowledge' in that, unlike most IB subjects, history has its own section in the TOK syllabus. Why history has its own section, whereas geography or biology, for example, do not, is part of what we look at in this chapter. In brief, history is special with its own very unique set of epistemological problems.

To your TOK teacher you are a history specialist. You have been studying history for a number of years and can therefore expect special attention when the TOK class comes around to study history as an 'area of knowledge'. You can anticipate being quizzed on the big epistemological questions: What exactly is history? Or how can we know what happened in the past? Or what is the point of studying history? If you have never considered these questions before, this is not your fault. It is a product of what the great English social historian Raphael Samuel once described as history's 'naive realism'.[1] As illustrated by J. H. Hexter's imaginary dialogue at the start of this chapter, historians like to do history; they don't tend to think much about how they do it.

But other than your academic street cred, what else can a serious approach to TOK history provide? Put simply, it will make you a more thoughtful and original history student. For example, the close (micro) document analysis of Paper 1 will benefit from a broader philosophical (macro) approach to what makes sources useful or reliable. An understanding of how history is written, where interpretations come from and why historians might disagree will help you in your essay writing for Papers 2 and 3. And most obviously, the major research assignments of the IA and extended essay will score much more highly if there is evidence of an original, self-reflective voice that is in control of both the narrative and the **methodology** behind the assignment. The books listed at the end of this chapter as suggested further reading will help you with this.

methodology: the systematic study of methods that are, can be or have been applied within a discipline, in this case history

This chapter is therefore not so concerned with giving you a guide to the history section of your TOK course, but rather bringing the TOK knowledge issues into your study of history. It urges you not just to do history but to think about it.

This section will address three issues:

- what history is and is not – how it is made and who makes it
- the epistemological weaknesses of history – the three inherent problems of trying to do history
- the value of history – how despite its weaknesses, good history is increasingly important in our post-modern world.

What history is and is not

History is not the past

In English we tend to use the words 'history' and 'the past' interchangeably and so cause a semantic problem. One of the most useful things you can do in studying history is to begin to use these words to signify very different things.

The **past** is a term used to indicate all the events which occurred before a given point in time: everything that has ever happened to everyone, everywhere at any time before now. The past is neither the present nor the future.

In contrast, **history** is a narrative text, written in the present, about the subject of the past, using evidence that the past has left behind. This is important because all history must be an interpretation of the past and never the 'same thing' as the past.

TOK prescribed essay title
Compare and contrast our approach to knowledge about the past with our approach to knowledge about the future.
November 2008/May 2009
© IB Organization

---

1 Samuel, R., 1990, quoted in Keith Jenkins, 1991, *Re-thinking History*, London: Routledge, p. 2.

How does something from the past become history?

If asked about the difference between 'history' and the 'past' you would probably think about significance. If asked to choose a historical event you will choose something historically significant, for example something that had an impact on the lives of lots of people or that caused something else important to happen. In contrast, if asked to choose an example of something from the past you might choose your last history lesson, which was of no wider significance and will not make it into the history books of the future.

- In pairs or groups, invent a scenario in which your next history lesson might become a historical event. Compare your scenario with those of the rest of the class. Are there any common themes in each of the scenarios?
- The US geographer David Lowenthal argued in 1985 that 'history is both more and less than the past'. What do you think he might have meant by this?

Lowenthal, D., 1985, *The Past is a Foreign Country*, Cambridge: Cambridge University Press.

History is both a process and a product

History is an activity that is done (a process of doing history) and an end result (a product of historical text). History is made (written) as a result of a highly skilled process known as doing history.

Historians will have spent many years after their undergraduate degree in history learning the skills of researching and writing history. If the product – a text about the past – is not a result of the highly skilled process, it is not history. This is important because anyone can tell stories about the past that may appear historical, but if the process used (methodology) is not historical, then it's not history.

> **TOK prescribed essay title**
> What similarities and differences are there between historical and scientific explanations?
> *November 2009/May 2010*
> © IB Organization

History is made by historians

You are not a historian and neither is the author of this chapter. Generally, history is done by historians working in a university history department. Many people may have similar qualifications to them and may do things that look similar – teach history, direct historical documentary films, work as curators in museums – but these people generally are not historians. This is important because although they may do many useful things with the past – teach children, inform a wider public, preserve documents – their primary purpose is not the same as the historian's. An IB history teacher's primary purpose will be to prepare students for the IB history examination; this is not what historians do.

History is both an art and a (social) science

This partly explains history's special position in the TOK programme and a number of its epistemological problems. Historians can use methodologies that resemble those of the most quantitative social sciences, for example cliometricians' computer-processed analysis of census data. Historians are just as likely, though, to use methods that require qualitative appreciation of things that cannot be measured, for example empathetic sensitivity to long-gone attitudes and opinions. Being a historian involves familiarity with a challengingly wide range of skills. This is important because historians may legitimately engage with the past in any number of ways and this will result in a very wide range of different types of history and interpretations.

cliometrics: the systematic application of economic theory or mathematical methods to the study of history, especially social and economic history

History is plural

Rather than history we should really be talking about histories. There are many possible interpretations to any event and to any period of history. As a history student looking out of a window you may see a medieval church with Gothic spires alongside a post-war town constructed from the ruins of bombing during the Second World War. In contrast a geographer looking at the same scene may draw attention to a river basin or an urban pattern that corresponds to a particular land-use model, while a biologist may be more interested in the spiders on a web just outside the window. The past is like view from the the window and historians may legitimately focus on any aspect of the view they wish. This is important because although historians are theoretically free to choose what they like, they tend to focus on similar things.

This introduces us to the question of the power behind history. History tends to reflect what the state and its educational institutions want it to reflect. Historical consensus about history (especially national history) is neither natural nor inevitable – it needs to be created and defended.

TOK prescribed essay title
"We see and understand things not as they are but as we are." Discuss this claim in relation to at least two ways of knowing.
November 2009/May 2010
© IB Organization

Activity

The power behind history

For although professional historians overwhelmingly present themselves as academic and disinterested, and although they are certainly in some ways 'distanced', nevertheless, it is more illuminating to see such practitioners as being not so much outside the ideological fray but as occupying very dominant positions within it; to see professional histories as expressions of how dominant ideologies currently articulate history 'academically'. It seems rather obvious that, seen in a wider cultural and 'historical' perspective, multi-million pound institutional investments such as our national universities are integral to the reproductions of the on-going social formation and are at the forefront of cultural guardianship (academic standards) and ideological control; it would be somewhat careless if they were not.

Jenkins, K., 1991, *Re-thinking History*, London: Routledge.

George Orwell famously argued in *1984*: 'Who controls the past controls the future: who controls the present controls the past.'

Orwell, G., 1948, *1984*, London, Secker and Warburg.

In the light of these comments from Jenkins and Orwell, list the reasons why history is a compulsory subject in most schools around the world.

The three epistemological problems of history

There are three distinct epistemological problems that relate to each of the three stages in the study of history:

- finding the raw material (the sources)
- interpreting the evidence (the method)
- writing the history text (the product).

Problem 1: the sources

> The Memory of the world is not a bright, shining crystal, but a heap of broken fragments, a few fine flashes of light that break through the darkness.
>
> Butterfield, H., 1924, *The Historical Novel*, Cambridge: Cambridge University Press, pg. 15.

Flawed raw materials

The first thing that makes historical knowledge difficult to acquire is the inadequacy of the raw materials that the historian is forced to work with. Unlike a social scientist, who can directly observe participants in a controlled experimental context, our inability to travel through time means that the historian relies on indirect and uncontrolled evidence – in the extract from Butterfield above, the 'heap of broken fragments'– that the past has left behind. Even more significantly, most of the past has left no evidence at all of what happened, it is simply unknowable – this is the 'darkness' that Butterfield refers to. Most people who have ever lived and most events that have ever happened left no record, no fragments from which historians might reconstruct a version of the past.

> **TOK prescribed essay title**
> 'The knowledge that we value the most is the knowledge for which we can provide the strongest justifications.' To what extent would you agree with this claim?
> *November 2009/May 2010*
> © IB Organization

Those records that do exist are often atypical or accidental. We may have sources deliberately left to posterity but that makes them unrepresentative. The same is true of sources that have survived centuries of fires, wars and revolutions. Historians also have to use sources never intended for future interpretation, accidental by-products of past events, unintended communiqués with the future. The evidence only speaks to historians indirectly, with no guarantee that it will answer their questions. As a consequence, historians must resign themselves to a patient trawl through records, most of which have no relevance to their needs.

Activity

Future implications of information technology on history

In a book of source skills for students produced in the early 1990s the historian Brian Brivati drew attention to the fact the telephone had reduced the tendency for people to write letters. He feared that because of this, future historians would be denied the rich resource that letter writing had provided for historians of previous generations. He concluded by hoping the recent invention of the fax machine might do much to reverse the situation but he was writing at a time before the advent of the internet.

- Will the Internet revolution of the past 20 years make easier or more difficult the job of 22nd century historians of the early 21st century?

Problem 2: the method

Antoine Roquetin, the historian in Jean-Paul Sartre's Nausea, says:

I am beginning to believe that nothing can ever be proved... slow, lazy, sulky, the facts adapt themselves at a pinch to the order I wish to give them.

Sartre, J. P., 1938, *La Nausée*, Paris: Galliard, pg. 26.

One of the key features of the scientific method depends on an ability to test theories by predictive experimentation. We can examine the importance of light as a cause of plant growth by examining two parallel plants, one in the light and one in the dark. But history lacks this ability to control the variables so essential to the scientific method. We cannot stop the car from making a wrong turning on 28 June 1914 to see if the First World War would have happened without the assassination of Franz Ferdinand.

All history can do is interpret; it constructs plausible meanings from the evidence that the past has left behind. But what this means in reality is two levels of interpretation.

The two levels of interpretation

The first level

In the first level of interpretation, historians depend entirely on the people who have interpreted the events they have lived through and who have left historians a record to consider. The process of making sense of the world, of committing thoughts to paper or a photograph to posterity is itself an interpretation.

One of best illustrations of this first level of interpretation is made by E. H. Carr in the classic introduction to the philosophy of history: *What is History?* Carr describes the archive of 'primary documents' left by the Weimar Germany's Foreign Minister Gustav Stresemann and the hundreds of diplomatic conversations he conducted. What do the documents tell us? 'They depict Stresemann as having the lion's share of the conversations and reveal his arguments as invariably well put and cogent, while those of his partner are for the most part scanty, confused and unconvincing. This is a familiar characteristic of all diplomatic conversations. The documents do not tell us what happened, but only what Stresemann thought had happened, or what he wanted others to think, or perhaps what he wanted himself to think, had happened.'

Carr, E. H., 1961, What is History?,(1986 edn.), London: Macmillan, pp. 12–13.

TOK prescribed essay title
When mathematicians, historians and scientists say that they have explained something, are they using the word 'explain' in the same way?
November 2006/May 2007
© IB Organization

Edward Hallett "Ted" Carr CBE (1892 –1982) was a left-wing British historian, journalist and diplomat. Carr was best known for his 14-volume history of the Soviet Union, in which he provided an account of Soviet history from 1917 to 1929, for his writings on international relations, and for his classic 1961 introduction to the study of the history, *What Is History?*

But it is not only that we cannot trust the eyes and ears of witnesses to tell us the truth about what happened, they cannot be trusted to tell the truth even to themselves. Social psychologists have explained through **cognitive dissonance theory** that individuals are prone to provide explanations for events that are at odds with their thinking at the time of the event. How can we know what people in the past thought if we cannot be certain that those people knew themselves?

The second level

The second stage of interpretation is the interpretation of the past evidence by the historians themselves. The historian gives the past meaning that the past itself cannot have had for those who lived through it. As Sir Herbert Butterfield once argued, the role of the historian is to understand the people of the past 'better than they understood themselves'.[2] Historians look back on the past seeing connections between events, the significance of events, and the patterns of cause and effect. It was impossible for those living through the events to see these aspects for themselves. As Margaret MacMillan has recently argued, 'The idea that those who actually took part in great events or lived through particular times have a superior understanding to those who came later is a deeply held yet wrong-headed one.'[3]

For example, nobody in 1917 could know how significant the Bolshevik Revolution was. Few expected Lenin's party to hold on to power for long and had the Bolsheviks lost the Civil War then the relative significance of the Revolution would have been different from what it became at the height of the Cold War in the 1950s. And now, 20 years after the end of the Cold War, the study of 1917 no longer seems to have the same urgency it once did, with the study of the history of China and the Middle East now seeming much more pertinent.

This is one of those odd features of history that people often struggle to understand – that history continues to change and evolve even though it's the same old past that is being described. Each generation writes its own history of the French Revolution or of the First World War. Why is this? The continual need to produce new histories of old subjects is partly explained by historians uncovering new evidence in the archives. For example, the periodic declassification of once secret government documents provides a regular supply of new materials that inevitably changes our earlier perspectives. A much more profound explanation for our need for new histories is to be found in the Italian philosopher Benedetto Croce's famous observation that 'All history is contemporary history.'

History is made by historians and what they write will therefore reflect both their personality and more importantly the times they are living in. This is illustrated by the extract below, from the Oxford historian A. L. Rowse's introductory text *The Use of History*, where he considers the role of history in the school curriculum.

Cognitive dissonance theory
A classical example of this idea (and the origin of the expression 'sour grapes') is expressed in the fable 'The Fox and the Grapes' by Aesop (ca. 620–564 BCE). In the story, a fox sees some high-hanging grapes and wants to eat them. When the fox is unable to think of a way to reach them, he assumes that the grapes are probably not worth eating, as they must not be ripe or must be sour.

TOK prescribed essay title
"People need to believe that order can be glimpsed in the chaos of events" (adapted from John Gray, Heresies, 2004). In what ways and to what extent would you say this claim is relevant in at least two areas of knowledge?
November 2009/May 2010
© IB Organization

TOK prescribed essay title
Discuss the claim that some areas of knowledge are discovered and others are invented.
November 2009/May 2010
© IB Organization

I think the royal road to appealing to the interest of the schoolboy... is the biographical: lives of great men, especially men of action, like the great English seamen or soldiers and adventurers and their exciting stories... Schoolboys respond immediately to the appeal of patriotism, to the spirit of self-devotion in such lives as Wolfe, Sir John Moore, Nelson, Livingstone, General Gordon, Scott of the Antarctic, Lawrence of Arabia. They feel the thrill of achievement in such careers as Clive's or Drake's or Rhodes'...

Rowse, A. L., 1927, *The Use of History*, London: Hodder and Stoughton, pg. 145.

2 Butterfield, H., 1931, *The Whig Interpretation of History*, (1959 edn.), London: Bell and Sons, p. 3.
3 MacMillan, M., 2009, *The Uses and Abuses of History*, London: Profile Books, pg. 44.

School history as patriotic storytelling of the lives of great, white English, empire-building men seems strangely archaic today. But it is his appeal to the school*boy* and not girl that does most to date Rowse to the early 20th century. Is he deliberately excluding girls in his choice of the word 'schoolboy'? On the role of science in school he is unambiguous, as shown in the extract below.

> ...I deeply doubt whether physics and chemistry have any educational value in girls' schools at all. I should have thought that in these their place might be more profitably taken, for obvious reasons, by biology, hygiene and natural history – sciences of life rather than of matter.
>
> Rowse, A. L., 1927, *The Use of History*, London: Hodder and Stoughton, pg. 145.

What is 'obvious' in the extract above – what needs no explanation – are the unconscious, hidden assumptions that make Rowse a man of his age, nationality and social class. History changed in the 20th century because historians stopped being exclusively men like Rowse.

The success of socialism, feminism and decolonization in the 20th century, broadened social and educational opportunities so that history today reflects the wider agenda of those the 20th century emancipated and empowered. During the 20th century, history became concerned with the working classes, women and ethnic minorities; groups that had been hidden from history and whose existence had been neglected.

TOK prescribed essay title
"History is always on the move, slowly eroding today's orthodoxy and making space for yesterday's heresy." Discuss the extent to which this claim applies to history and at least one other area of knowledge.
November 2007/May 2008
© IB Organization

The National
Women's
History Project

WOMEN'S HISTORY MONTH

The problems with the historian's method are therefore profound. In summary: knowledge of the past is always mediated through two levels of interpretation and history is always a work in progress reflecting both the discovery of new evidence and the changing attitudes of historians.

Women's' History Month has taken place in March every year since its foundation in the 1970s, timed to correspond with International Women's Day on the 8th of March. It is an event that highlights contributions of women to events in history and contemporary society.

Activity

Writing your own 'histories'
Each member of your class should produce his or her own individual 'history' of today. Other than a word limit, of say 500 words, no other requirements should be specified. When you have completed your 'history', compare and contrast it with the work of other students. In your analysis consider both the form and content of the 'histories' produced, as follows.

- Form: How many of the 'histories' were written accounts? How many used approximately 500 words? How many were chronological? How were sentences and paragraphs structured? Was there an introduction and conclusion?

- Content: How many of the 'histories' were just descriptive? How many students included how they felt? How many included opinions and judgments? How many included supporting factual evidence? How many included a description of today's history lesson? How many included events outside their personal experience, for example international events?

Then move on to answer these questions.

- Why were so many accounts similar in both form and content?
- How and why did the accounts differ?
- Why did the history lesson feature in so many of the 'histories'?
- What problems would you face if you tried to write a history of the same day a year earlier?
- Were any of the 'histories' more truthful than others?
- Were any of the 'histories' better than others?

Problem 3: the product

> 'We won't understand a thing about human life if we persist in avoiding the most obvious fact: that a reality no longer is what it was; it cannot be reconstructed.'
>
> Kundera, M. (trs. Asher, L.), 2002, *Ignorance*, Paris: Gallimard, pg. 123.

Two difficulties – comparison and verification

The third epistemological problem of history stems from the simple inability to be able to compare like with like. History cannot be compared to the past and cannot be verified against the past, because the past and history are different things. This is one of the key means that philosophers use to verify knowledge and that you may come across this in your TOK lessons as **correspondence theory**.

The historical text, the narrative account, can never reconstruct the past as it was, because the past was not a text, it was a series of events, experiences, situations and so on. If someone drew a picture of you and then took a photograph from exactly the same position it is very likely that the photograph would provide the more reliable indication of what you look like 'in reality'. But when a historian writes an account of the past, all there is to compare it with are other written accounts, whether contemporary or historical. History has no absolute or 'objective reality'[4] to compare itself to, only other texts.

correspondence theory: this theory of truth states that the truth or falsity of a statement is determined only by how it relates to the world, and whether it accurately describes (that is, corresponds with) the world

Bringing the past alive

So in the absence of an 'objective reality' to judge against, what does our society consider to be good history? Factual accuracy is assumed and does not in itself constitute good history. Read the reviews of the latest historical bestseller and they do not commend the author for 'getting the dates right' or for 'putting events in chronological order'. Much more likely is praise for the historian's 'depth of research' or his or her ability to 'bring the past alive'. If archival research constitutes the social-scientific craft of the historian, then

---

4 Levi-Strauss, C. '... historical fact has no objective reality; it only exists as ... retrospective reconstruction', 1965, quoted in David Lowenthal, 1985, *The Past is a Foreign Country*, Cambridge: Cambridge University Press, pg. 215.

bringing the past alive relies on the historian's art; a creative, artistic ability that is rarely acknowledged. If history is just a text, its artistic effectiveness must rely upon the same skills that make all literature 'good' whether factual or fictional. Consider the following extract from one of the most celebrated recent historians of the Russian Revolution, Orlando Figes, as he describes the events of Bloody Sunday 1905.

TOK prescribed essay title
Can literature "tell the truth" better than other Arts or Areas of Knowledge?
November 2006/May 2007
© IB Organization

Orlando Figes (b.1959) is Professor of History at Birkbeck, University of London. He is known for his works on Russian history, in particular *A People's Tragedy* (1996), *Natasha's Dance* (2002) and *The Whisperers* (2007).

Snow had fallen in the night and St Petersburg awoke to an eerie silence on that Sunday morning, 9 January 1905. Soon after dawn the workers and their families congregated in churches to pray for a peaceful end to the day… Singing hymns and carrying icons and crosses, they formed something more like a religious procession than a workers' demonstration. Bystanders took off their hats and crossed themselves as they passed. And yet there was no doubt that the marchers' lives were in danger… Church bells rang and their golden domes sparkled in the sun on that Sunday morning as the long columns marched across the ice towards the centre of the city. In the front ranks were the women and children, dressed in their Sunday best, who had been placed there to deter the soldiers from shooting. At the head of the largest column was the bearded figure of Father Gapon in a long white cassock carrying a crucifix. Behind him was a portrait of the Tsar and a large white banner with the words: 'Soldiers do not shoot at the people!' Red flags had been banned… Suddenly, a bugle sounded and the soldiers fired into the crowd. A young girl, who had climbed up on to an iron fence to get a better view, was crucified to it by the hail of bullets. A small boy, who had mounted the equestrian statue of Prince Przewalski, was hurled into the air by a volley of artillery. Other children were hit and fell from the trees where they had been perching… When the firing finally stopped and the survivors looked around at the dead and wounded bodies on the ground there was one vital moment, the turning-point of the whole revolution, when their mood suddenly changed from disbelief to anger…

Figes, O., 1998, *A People's Tragedy: The Russian Revolution, 1891–1924*, Harmondsworth: Penguin, pp. 173–179.

Working with imaginative text

Strip back Figes' account to its factual essentials – a list of events in chronological order – and what are we left with? Other than the chronologically determined facts that make up the raw material of history, everything else – selective emphasis, anecdote, poetic scene setting, dramatic structure of the story, figurative language, moral judgement and significance 'the turning point of the whole revolution'– all come from the imagination of the historian.

This third epistemological problem is therefore perhaps the most profound of all. History is a largely imaginative text that cannot be verified against absolute reality, but only against other imaginative texts. Chronology and factual accuracy are not in themselves history. The extract below is from Hayden White, the most influential commentator on the problem.

> The events must be not only registered within the chronological framework of their original occurrence but narrated as well, that is to say, revealed as possessing a structure, an order of meaning, that they do not possess as mere sequence.
>
> White, H. V., 1990, *The Content of the Form*, Baltimore, MA: John Hopkins University Press, pg. 5.

TOK prescribed essay title
Compare the roles played by reason and imagination in at least two Areas of Knowledge.
November 2006/May 2007
© IB Organization

Activity

Post-modernism and the challenge to history

In battling against people who would subject historical studies to the dictates of literary critics we historians are, in a way, fighting for our lives. Certainly, we are fighting for the lives of innocent young people beset by devilish tempters who claim to offer higher forms of thought and deeper truths and insights – the intellectual equivalent of crack.

Elton, G., quoted in Richard J. Evans, 1997, *In Defence of History*, London: Granta Books, pg. 7.

The section above on the three epistemological problems of history has relied heavily on the 'post-modern' critique of history that has emerged over the last 30 years or so. In that sense we have played the role of what Elton described above as a 'devilish tempter'. Post-modernism is a general intellectual movement that has influenced most academic disciplines, but of particular relevance to history is the view that language is not simply an objective reflection of reality (the 'linguistic turn'). For some historians, such as Elton, the post-modern contention that historians create meaning as much as discover it, is a dangerous threat to a subject that aspires to Ranke's ideal of finding out 'what really happened' from the sources of the past themselves.

Before reading the last section of this chapter consider the following. One of criticisms levelled at post-modernism is that of 'relativism', that in the absence of absolute certainty, 'anything goes'. How would you reassure Elton that despite history's epistemological problems, history can be done and should be done by historians still using more or less the same methods as they have always used?

TOK prescribed essay title
`It is more important to discover new ways of thinking about what is already known than to discover new data or facts'. To what extent would you agree with this claim?
November 2006/May 2007
© IB Organization

The value of history: its uses and abuses

> I used to think that the profession of history, unlike that of, say, nuclear physics, could at least do no harm. Now I know it can. Our studies can turn into bomb factories... We have a responsibility to historical facts in general, and for criticizing the politico-ideological abuse of history in particular.
>
> Hobsbawm, E., 1998, *On History*, London: Abacus Books, pg. 7.

Having reviewed the main aspects of history's difficulties in finding out and explaining what happened in the past, it is important to conclude with a review of why, despite these epistemological difficulties, the academic study of the past and the profession of the historian remain so very important.

Good history is not heritage

The past can be used for almost anything you want to do in the present. We abuse it when we create lies about the past or write histories that show only one perspective.

Macmillan, M., 2010, *The Uses and Abuses of History*, London: Profile Books, pg. xiii.

The goal of the good historian is to try and find out what really happened. Not everyone who uses the past has such noble ambitions, though. What makes historians special users of the past is that they alone are concerned with making sense of the past, simply for the sake of making sense of the past. History is the study of the past in itself, for itself.

David Lowenthal makes a useful distinction on this point: he says that if users of the past are using the past for present-day purposes – whether positive, benign or harmful – then what they are doing is not history, but rather 'heritage' (see the extract below).

'...heritage is not history at all; while it borrows from and enlivens historical study, heritage is not an inquiry into past but a celebration of it, not an effort to know what actually happened but a profession of faith in a past tailored to present day purposes.'

Lowenthal, D, 1998 (second edn.), *The Heritage Crusade and Spoils of History*, Cambridge: Cambridge University Press, pg. x.

Never has our interest in heritage and our 'profession of faith in the past', been as fanatical as it is at the start of the 21st century. The past provides stability and certainty in a time of unprecedented social and cultural change: the past is everywhere – on dedicated television channels and in hundreds of successful Hollywood films, heritage sites, folklore celebrations, glossy magazines, bestselling novels and nostalgic commercial advertisements. They may borrow from history and may even be produced by historians, but they share a common non-historical, *present*-oriented purpose: they are there to entertain, to inspire, to engage, to provide identity and to sell to us, in the here and now.

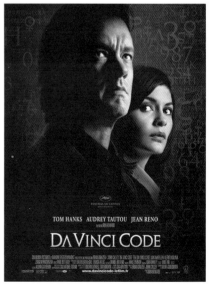

The past and national identity

As the past is central to our emotional sense of identity, the state has always sought to control how we interpret the past through, for example, national memorials, public holidays and the teaching of history in schools. As Arthur Marwick once explained, 'As memory is to the individual, so history is to the community'.[5] A shared sense of the past is central to our national identity

---

5 Marwick, A., 1989, *The Nature of History*, London: Macmillan, pg. 14.

because the nation is in Benedict Anderson's phrase 'an imagined community'.[6] It is also an exclusive community, though; national 'history' is *our* history, often defined in terms of opposition to those outside the national group. Only historians stand in the way of those who use the past as part of a patriotic agenda, because only historians have the means to, and interest in, exposing partiality and challenging the myths that often constitute the national story.

Good history, therefore, is one in which historians are 'open about their closures'; consciously aware of their present-oriented prejudices, both cultural and personal, but determined to remove this from all aspects of their work.

Activity

School history textbooks

In many parts of the world, the content of the history curriculum and writing of history textbooks is a carefully controlled, politically sensitive operation. For example, recent controversies over history textbooks in Japan became a significant diplomatic incident. In contrast, in 2006, former wartime enemies France and Germany brought out a common textbook written by authors from both countries and used in schools in both countries at the equivalent of IB Diploma level.

Research the textbook controversies in Japan and other countries such as Greece, Russia and Romania. What made the textbooks so contentious?

Have you or any friends had experience of a national history curriculum? Have you still got a textbook you can bring in to class? From your own experience consider history topics that are common or compulsory in your national curriculum, but unlikely to be found in a textbook of a neighbouring country.

TOK prescribed essay title
To understand something you need to rely on your own experience and culture. Does this mean that it is impossible to have objective knowledge?
November 2008/May 2009
© IB Organization

6 Anderson, B., 1991, *Imagined Communities: Reflections on the origin and spread of nationalism*, London, Verso Books.

Good history is not easy

> ...there is no doubt that the old history, traditional history, is hard. Hard – but exciting precisely because it is hard.
>
> Himmelfarb, G., 'Telling it as you like it: postmodernist history and the flight from fact', quoted in Keith Jenkins (ed.), 1997, *The Postmodern History Reader*, London: Routledge, pg. 173.

Tasks that make history hard

What you are learning to do in IB history Paper 1, to analyse and evaluate sources, is not easy. Writing essays for Papers 2 and 3, structuring a coherent account about the past that is persuasive and well supported by the facts, is intellectually challenging. The IB expects the extended essays and IAs to be fully referenced with sources acknowledged and this is a highly time-consuming process. You may not be a historian, but you are beginning to replicate the skills that historians use.

Real history is hard going: it is a methodical, sometimes lonely existence of reading, checking and double checking, of immersing yourself in the past and trying to empathize with the dead, of writing up carefully and reaching qualified judgements scrupulously, while providing explicit, accurate references for everything you write. As the French author Flaubert once said, 'Writing history is like drinking an ocean and pissing a cupful.'

The US historian William Dunning discovered through careful archival research and comparison of handwriting that Andrew Jackson's first message to Congress had in fact been drafted by George Bancroft. How much time must this comparison have taken? How many samples of handwriting had Dunning reviewed? The end result is relatively trivial but central to the historical process because 'it is not only new it is also true.'[7] The uncovering of new truths is a significant part of what history does. It is a cumulative process and over time we come to know more about the past than we once did.

It is far easier not to bother with monotonous archival research or to write about the past as if the people of the past were just like us. It is far easier not to provide detailed footnotes or to just select the lessons of the past because they suit our present needs. When those in positions of political power or economic influence tell stories about the past to justify their actions, it is only the professionally trained historian who has the real authority to challenge them. This is something else that can make history hard, that historians play the role of professional sceptics, often charged with being unpatriotic or disloyal. For those in power and defending the status quo, history can be a dangerous subject that teaches that the world hasn't always been like this, that change has happened and by implication can happen again.

<aside>
TOK prescribed essay title
Examine the ways empirical evidence should be used to make progress in different areas of knowledge.
© IB Organization
</aside>

---

7 Himmelfarb, G., 'Telling it as you like it: postmodernist history and the flight from fact', quoted in Keith Jenkins (ed.), 1997, *The Postmodern History Reader*, London: Routledge, pg. 173.

Tony Blair and Iraq – Learning the lessons of history

In a comparison likely to inflame the anti-war camp, he [British Prime Minister Tony Blair] said that appeasers in the 1930s had been decent people but had turned out to be wrong... 'When people decided not to confront fascism, they were doing the popular thing, they were doing it for good reasons, and they were good people ... but they made the wrong decision... I've never claimed to have a monopoly of wisdom, but one thing I've learned in this job is you should always try to do the right thing, not the easy thing. Let the day-to-day judgments come and go: be prepared to be judged by history.'

The *Guardian*, 1 March 2003

Was Tony Blair justified in comparing his decision to go to war in Iraq with policy of appeasing dictators in 1930s Europe?

What do think Blair meant when he said that he will be 'judged by history?'

TOK prescribed essay title

Discuss the ways in which value judgments should and should not be used in different Areas of Knowledge.

November 2007/May 2008

© IB Organization

Good history is not fiction

We historians are firmly bound by the authority of our sources (and by no other authority, human or divine), nor must we use fiction to fill in the gaps...

Elton, G., 'Return to essentials', quoted in Keith Jenkins (ed.), 1997, *The Postmodern History Reader*, London: Routledge, pg. 179.

Pursuing the facts

Finally, and above all else, history is concerned with facts about real events that actually happened. Events cannot be invented that did not happen, nor can the chronology of these events be reversed. There are real limitations to the narratives that can be told about the past and those limitations are fixed by the facts. There was a revolution in Cuba before the Cuban Missile Crisis and a year later President Kennedy was assassinated. As the historian G. M. Trevelyan once argued '...the poetry of history does not consist of imagination roaming at large, but of imagination pursuing the fact and fastening upon it.'[8]

For any claim historians make about the past they must provide evidential support from the historical record. And the historian must be open and accurate about this. The historian must provide clear referencing to allow the authenticity of the original source to be verified and to allow his or her interpretative reading of these sources to be analysed.

The integrity of the archive:

the strange case of historian Martin Allen

Martin Allen is a British historian who wrote a series of controversial books beginning in 2000 with *Hidden Agenda*, a work that claimed that the Duke of Windsor, former King Edward VIII, secretly aided the Nazis during the Second World War. In 2005 Allen wrote *Himmler's Secret War* which among other things accused Churchill's government of assassinating Himmler to stop him revealing that the British had secretly discussed peace terms with the Nazis without informing the USA or USSR.

Then in 2005, following an investigation by journalists, it was found that Allen's books were based on 29 forged documents that had been recently 'placed' in

8 Himmelfarb, G., *op. cit.*, pg. 166.

the British National Archives. The 1945 documents had been created on a high-resolution laser printer (invented in the 1970s). Signatures were found to be written over pencil tracings. Handwriting of different officials was suspiciously similar. Diplomatic titles and key dates were wrong. The police were called in and a criminal case was prepared, but then the case was dropped on the grounds that a trial would not be in the public interest. Allan is reportedly 'devastated' by the discovery of the forgeries and claims he was set up. The Internet is awash with conspiracy theories about the possible reasons why the criminal case was dropped.

In response to the decision to drop the prosecution a group of leading historians sent a letter to *The Financial Times* demanding an official public report of the case. Why do you think historians were so upset that forgeries had been found in the National Archive? What arguments do you think they used to try and persuade the government to hold an inquiry?

Before looking the case up on the Internet, consider what sorts of conspiracy theories you think might exist about the 'real' reasons for dropping the case against Martin Allen.

Beware some published accounts

One of the negative consequences of the Internet revolution has been decline in importance of the academic authority that was once more or less guaranteed by the published book. Now anyone can publish their views about the past on a website, blog or discussion board, whether they have respected the traditional requirements of academic historical scholarship or not. Conspiracy theory websites of variable quality rank highly in search results alongside reputable institutional history sites. Politically motivated sites can promote selective nationalist history and revisionist sites can, for example, deny that the Holocaust ever happened. In the face of such narratives it is not enough that there are simply alternative narratives. There must also be accounts that are founded on the factual record. For these accounts we depend on history. This is illustrated below by Richard J. Evans' forceful argument about the Holocaust.

> **TOK prescribed essay title**
> "Context is all" (Margaret Atwood). Does this mean that there is no such thing as truth?
> November 2007/May 2008
> © IB Organization

> There is a massive, carefully empirical literature on the Nazi extermination of the Jews. Clearly, to regard it as fictional, unreal, or no nearer to historical reality than, say, the work of the 'revisionists' who deny that Auschwitz ever happened at all, is simply wrong. Here is an issue where evidence really counts, and can be used to establish the essential facts. Auschwitz was not a discourse. It trivializes mass murder to see it as a text. The gas chambers were not a piece of rhetoric. Auschwitz was inherently a tragedy and cannot be seen either as a comedy or a farce.
>
> Evans, R. J., 1997, *In Defence of History*, London: Granta Books, pg. 124.

Activity

Why does it matter if people do not know about the past?

A conversation overheard in a New York bar, 11 September 2001 went like this.

Man 1: 'This is just like Pearl Harbor.'

Man 2: 'What is Pearl Harbor?'

Man 1: 'That was when the Vietnamese dropped bombs in a harbour, and it started the Vietnam War.'

Macmillan, M., 2009, *The Uses and Abuses of History*, London: Profile Books, pg. 165.

There are many people, politicians and business leaders among them, who feel that too much time is dedicated to history in the school curriculum that could be used to teach more 'useful' or 'relevant' subjects such as ICT or business studies. In a group, prepare a 5-minute presentation or film that demonstrates the continued importance of history in the school curriculum.

Activity

Historians with 'bees in their bonnets'

'Study the historian before you begin to study the facts. This is, after all, not very abstruse. It is what is already done by the intelligent undergraduate who, when recommended to read a work by that great scholar Jones of St. Jude's, goes round to a friend at St. Jude's to ask what sort of chap Jones is, and what bees he has in his bonnet. When you read a work of history, always listen out for the buzzing. If you can detect none, either you are tone deaf or your historian is a dull dog.'

EH Carr What is History? pp 17-18

One of the major criticisms from IB history examiners is that history students tend to consider historiography as little more than 'name-dropping' historians. As examiners report every year, being familiar with the names of historians does nothing to improve the quality of an essay. In contrast, knowing a little about how and why an historian has produced an important work and why that work is considered significant can be very useful. Obviously you cannot be expected to research every historian you come across, but for major historiographical debates that you study or for historians that are important to your Internal Assessment or Extended Essay, getting to know a little about the 'great scholars' can be very informative. Occasionally you may be lucky enough to come across one of these historians as one of the documents in Paper 1. Knowing a little about the historian's research or their life and times can help you get to grips with their motivation and possible biases. This will help you to stand out from students who rely on generic comments about the strengths and weaknesses of historians as sources of information about the past. And with the advent of the Internet it has never been easier to follow EH Carr's famous advice to 'study the historian before you begin to study the facts'.

Historian's significance	Archival research	Life and times

In the first column you should explain how and why the historian or their history has made an important contribution. If the historian has produced an important work based on new research about the past, you explain this is the second column. In the last column you can consider how the context in which the historian is working (political, personal, professional etc.) has contributed to the new way of interpreting the past. In the end you can judge whether the new development in the debate has come about primarily as a result of new research or the times in which the historian is writing.

References

Allen, M., 2002, *Hidden Agenda: How the Duke of Windsor betrayed the allies*, London: Pan Macmillan.

Anderson, B., 1991, *Imagined Communities: Reflections on the origin and spread of nationalism*, London: Verso.

Brivati, B., 'Private papers' in Peter Catterall and Harriet Jones,1994, *Understanding Documents and Sources,* Oxford: Heinemann.

Butterfield, H., 1924, *The Historical Novel,* Cambridge: Cambridge University Press.

Butterfield, H., 1931, *The Whig Interpretation of History,* (1959 edn.), London: Bell and Sons.

Carr, E. H., 1961, *What is History?,* (1986 edn.), London: Macmillan.

Evans, R. J., 1997, *In Defence of History*, London: Granta Books.

Figes, O., 1998, *A People's Tragedy: The Russian Revolution, 1891–1924*, Harmondsworth: Penguin.

Hobsbawm, E., 1998, *On History*, London: Abacus Books.

Jenkins, K., (ed.) 1997, *The Postmodern History Reader,* London: Routledge.

Jenkins, K., 1991, *Re-thinking History*, London: Routledge.

Kundera, M. (trs. Asher, L.), 2002, *Ignorance*, Paris: Gallimard.

Lowenthal, D., 1998 (second edn.), *The Heritage Crusade and Spoils of History*, Cambridge: Cambridge University Press.

Lowenthal, D., 1985, *The Past is a Foreign Country*, Cambridge: Cambridge University Press.

Macmillan, M., 2009, *The Uses and Abuses of History*, London: Profile Books.

Marwick, A., 1989, *The Nature of History*, London: Macmillan.

Orwell, G., 1948, *1984*, London, Secker and Warburg.

Rowse, A. L., 1927, *The Use of History*, London: Hodder and Stoughton.

Sartre, J. P., 1938, *La Nausée*, Paris: Galliard.

White, H. V., 1990, *The Content of the Form*, Baltimore, MA: John Hopkins University Press

Further reading

Evans, R. J., 1997, *In Defence of History*, London: Granta Books. (A highly respected historian takes time out to research and take seriously the post-modern attack on history. This is his often brilliant response.)

Jenkins, K., *Re-thinking History*, 1991, London: Routledge. (This is 70 pages of polemic, written in an informal, idiosyncratic style, that has produced a wide-range of often very emotional responses from the historical community.)

Lowenthal, D., 1985, *The Past is a Foreign Country*, Cambridge: Cambridge University Press. (A highly entertaining book that provides an encyclopaedic overview of how the past is used and abused and interestingly, why it is.)

Macmillan, M., 2009, *The Uses and Abuses of History*, London: Profile Books. (Based on a series of recent lectures given by the widely respected Canadian historian, this provides many good up-to-date examples of uses and abuses.)

Warren, J., 1999, *History and Historians*, London: Hodder and Stoughton. (A wonderfully concise history of history and very accessible; includes a very clear, relatively sympathetic overview of recent developments in the study of what is history.)

Jones-Nerzic, R - International School History www.internationalschoolhistory.net (Includes an expanded, hypertext version of this chapter)